Penguin Books
Babies Need Books

Dorothy Butler first became interested in the subject of children and their reading while teaching English in a secondary school. Her interest was focused on the pre-school years when her own children (she has six daughters and two sons) were small, and she became involved with the work of the Play Centre Association in New Zealand. As her children grew up she started her own business from home, selling children's books and providing an advisory service for parents. This expanded so rapidly that she was soon forced to move to larger premises and the business has continued to flourish ever since.

She was awarded the Diploma in Education of the University of Auckland for her study of her severely handicapped granddaughter, Cushla, and the crucial part that books have played in her development; this has subsequently been adapted for publication under the title *Cushla and Her Books* (Penguin 1987). She has also written a sequel to *Babies Need Books* entitled *Five to Eight* and published in 1986.

Dorothy Butler continues to run her highly successful children's bookshop in Auckland. She lectures and writes about children's books, is active in New Zealand children's publishing, and still manages to enjoy time spent with her eight grandsons, nine granddaughters and the rest of her large family.

DOROTHY BUTLER

Babies Need
Books

SECOND EDITION

with drawings by
Shirley Hughes

PENGUIN BOOKS

PENGUIN BOOKS

Published by the Penguin Group
27 Wrights Lane, London w8 5TZ, England
Viking Penguin Inc., 40 West 23rd Street, New York, New York 10010, USA
Penguin Books Australia Ltd, Ringwood, Victoria, Australia
Penguin Books Canada Ltd, 2801 John Street, Markham, Ontario, Canada L3R 1B4
Penguin Books (NZ) Ltd, 182–190 Wairau Road, Auckland 10, New Zealand

Penguin Books Ltd, Registered Offices: Harmondsworth, Middlesex, England

First published by The Bodley Head 1980
Published in Pelican Books 1982
Reprinted 1982, 1984
Second edition
published in Penguin Books 1988

Made and printed in Great Britain by
Richard Clay Ltd, Bungay, Suffolk
Filmset in 10 on 12pt Monophoto Baskerville

For Roy

Acknowledgements

I am grateful to Methuen Children's Books Ltd and to the Canadian Publishers, McClelland & Stewart Ltd, Toronto, for permission to use lines from A. A. Milne's poem 'The End' from *Now We Are Six* as headings for Chapters 3, 4, 5 and 6; and to G. P. Putnam's Sons for the Poem 'Little' by Dorothy Aldis for the heading to Chapter 2. The poem is reprinted from *All Together* by permission of the publishers, copyright 1925, 1926, 1927, 1928, 1934, 1939, 1952; renewed 1953, 1954, 1955, 1956, 1962, 1967 by Dorothy Aldis.

My thanks are also due to the publishers who have supplied information about books mentioned in the text. My publishers have done their best to ensure that all details and attributions are correct; however, any errors will naturally be rectified in any future reprint.

D.B.

Contents

Preface to the
Second Edition

'Under the sun there's nothing new,' said King Solomon, and he must have had babies in mind. The present crop in my own family is just as wide-eyed, captivating, maddening and rewarding as infants have always been.

Babies' *needs* haven't altered fundamentally either, in the near three thousand years since the great king's reflection. But the world that children must make sense of, and ultimately make their way through, has changed dramatically. Most of the change has taken place in the last hundred years, and relates of course to the technological revolution which has engulfed people's lives in that brief spell of world history. Even in the seven years that have elapsed since this book's first publication, the pace of change has accelerated.

Babies and children need, more than ever before, adults to love them, care for them, laugh with them, and help them to learn. But many adults themselves find the world a bewildering place in which to function. Meeting children's needs, even if these can be identified, may seem impossibly difficult. As never before, parents need encouragement, information and support.

This new edition has been revised, but not, in essence, changed. Its intention is still to offer help to parents and others who have the daily care of babies and young children. More than two hundred titles have been added, and as many deleted. It is a sad fact that no publisher these days can afford to keep a book in print if its sales do not justify its continued existence. There have been hundreds of casualties over the past decade.

I have none the less left a few out-of-print titles intact in the lists. This reflects my stubborn belief that a good book will, like a wandering son or daughter, surely return. Geoffrey Trease, a fine author for older children, said more than twenty years ago, 'If "out of print" came to mean "unmentionable" many a good book would never be rescued from the limbo into which it had temporarily fallen.' I hold fast to this belief and have, indeed, seen many such a book resurface after years of out-of-print obscurity. Clearly, keeping a fine book alive in people's memories is worth while, and sometimes pays off.

I can safely say that my new recommendations have all been tried and tested. But some of the old books are still the best. To have a daughter confirm that *Caps for Sale* is still two-and-a-half-year-old Joseph's favourite story, ahead of all the glossy, however beautiful, new books, reassures me that story reigns supreme, and that children are the ultimate judges. If we offer them the best, they will come to recognize it unconsciously, and be nourished by it. In short, they will become readers.

Introduction

I believe that books should play a prominent part in children's lives from babyhood; that access to books, through parents and other adults, greatly increases a child's chances of becoming a happy and involved human being.

The dedicated involvement of parents and other adults is, of course, an essential part of the process. Without the help of adults, a baby or small child has no chance at all of discovering books, of starting on the road to that unique association with the printed word which the mature reader knows and loves.

It is in the hope of persuading parents and others of the truth of this proposition that I have written this book. I want it to be of use to parents in much the same way as a car manual is of use to the motorist who aspires to give personal care and attention to his vehicle.

Fortunately, this need not mean encumbering parents with yet another onerous duty. Children's books these days are things of beauty and delight. The adult who becomes convinced that he should share them with his children has presented himself with a passport to fun, quite apart from the opportunity to stay in touch with his children through the years when their minds are daily expanding.

Children are, of course, different from cars. In an extremity, you can hand your car over to the care of an expert mechanic and be reasonably sure that his attention and skill will solve your problems. Delegation does not work so well for the young child. As society is now constituted, no agent seems to be as effective with the very young human being as one loving adult. Two, if possible, but one certainly.

A reassuring truth, in these days of increasing female involvement in the world outside the home, is that quality, not quantity, is the keynote of any relationship. Any two partners profit from a break, and this is as true of parent and child as it is of two adults. Over-exposure to the developing young, however well-loved they be, can lead to irritation (if not desperation!), with all the damaging effects this implies for both parties.

But a note of caution must be struck; if contact-hours are to be reduced, ways must be found for parents and children to experience one another joyfully during the time they are together.

It is my belief that there is no 'parents' aid' which can compare with the book in its capacity to establish and maintain a relationship with a child. Its effects extend far beyond the covers of the actual book, and invade every aspect of life. Parents and children who share books come to share the same frame of reference. Incidents in everyday life constantly remind one or the other – or both, simultaneously – of a situation, a character, an action, from a jointly enjoyed book, with all the generation of warmth and well-being that is attendant upon such sharing.

A great deal is written and said these days about the breakdown of communication between adolescents and their parents. All around us we hear adults complaining:

'He never tells us anything.'

'She doesn't even want to know what we think about anything.'

'Discuss the problem with him? You must be joking!'

In most of these cases, the give-and-take of shared opinion and ideas has never been practised before adolescence. The only reason some parents ultimately want to talk with their sons and daughters is that a very real problem has arisen. Adolescence is certainly the time for real problems – problems that can't be ignored, concealed, or smoothed over. But all too often, a parent is the very last person to whom the adolescent wants to talk. Not only has the line of communication never been set up, but all sorts of tensions and awkwardness have.

All this can be avoided by the early forging of relationships, by establishing the habit of verbal give-and-take. This does not mean that problems won't arise. It merely means that the human beings concerned will have ways of coping with difficulties, ways which may lead to the deepening rather than the damaging of relationships.

And books can play a major part in this process. Because by their very nature they are rooted in language, and because language is essential to human communication, and communication is the life blood of relationships, books *matter*.

Well then: How do we introduce books to babies? Which books? When? There may be some rare individuals who can cope unaided when they decide to adopt a new approach, but most of us are mere mortals, and need help. I will remember my own 'groping' days as a young parent. I know that I made mistakes, worried and felt guilty (often about the wrong things), steeled myself to behave in ways that were later revealed as not only useless but potentially damaging . . . and that always, always, in every area of parenthood, I could have used more informed advice than seemed available.

I'm still learning. My grandchildren keep teaching me things about small children that my own children left untaught, not least in the field of language and books. My love for them is tinged with gratitude, and constant wonder.

If this book can offer a little support to adults who are a bit further back on the learning trail in the book field than I am, I shall be pleased.

ABOUT THIS BOOK

I've made Chapter 1 a 'Why?' chapter, in case anyone reading this is sceptical of the whole proposition: that is, that involvement with books from babyhood is one of the greatest blessings and benefits that can come to any child.

If you are convinced of this already, and merely seek advice about ways, means and materials, you may prefer to begin with Chapter 2, which plunges into the mechanics of the thing. But read Chapter 1 later, if only to fortify yourself for encounters with sceptical friends.

The Book Lists between the chapters are to be regarded as important sections of the whole. Long lists are very daunting, so I have selected titles with great care. Nothing is included which I have not used myself with babies or small children. I have tried to describe each in such a way that you will understand my reason for suggesting it, and the way in which you might use it.

It goes without saying that there are other books available which might do just as well. I make no apology for including *my* favourite books, and hope that you will compile your own list in the years ahead.

A list is useless if you cannot get hold of the titles it suggests. The following details are intended to help you to use the Book Lists in a practical way; that is, to get your hands on any particular book that you want to try out with your child.

To begin with, note the details given about any book carefully. Title, author and publisher are the most important. If you are not familiar with these terms, examine the title-page at the beginning of this book. The title-page gives the full title, and the names of author, illustrator and publisher. In this case, you will see 'PEN-GUIN BOOKS' at the foot of the title-page. The publisher's name, sometimes in abbreviated form, or their logo (in this case, the Penguin) will also be found on the spine of the book. Compare the two if you need to check.

On the copyright page, which is usually found on the back of the title-page, are printed the full address of the publisher and the printer's name. The latter is not important in obtaining a book. Understanding the difference between publisher and printer may help you to avoid confusing them. The publisher creates the book. He either engages an author to write it, or accepts a manuscript already written. In either case, he works with the author to get the book into suitable form for publication. He arranges for illustrations if necessary, designs the layout, and manages all the business details. Then he sends the whole thing to a printer, who uses sophisticated modern machinery to print it. Last of all, it is bound into covers, and delivered to the publishers, who must then distribute it to booksellers and try to make sure that people know of its existence. The printer is no longer involved at this stage.

Let's assume, then, that you have noted the details of a particular title, and understand their significance. The next step is to ask at your library, giving all these details. Your librarian will find the requested title by reference to either title or author if the library owns it already. Libraries are often happy to buy a requested title if they do not already have it, in which case they will be helped by knowing the publisher and the International Standard Book Number, or ISBN. Since 1970, every book published in the world has been given its own ISBN; you may find *this* book's ISBN on the spine and the back cover.

You may decide that you want to buy the book, either before or after borrowing it from the library. A well-stocked children's bookshop should have most of the suggested titles in stock, and you may find it more convenient to browse in a bookshop. If the bookshop does *not* have your title in stock and you want to order it, the bookseller will need to know the publisher's name. A really considerate customer provides all three vital facts – title; author; publisher – and may even know the ISBN. A really considerate bookseller, of course, will have catalogues, directories, and perhaps even electronic equipment to help him find elusive titles. Better still, he may have human qualities of imagination, determination and interest.

Some years ago a customer rushed into our bookshop. She had just heard a radio review of 'a wonderful new children's book called *Daniel's Garden*' and she wanted to buy it for her small daughter. We had never let her down yet – she knew we would have it . . . We gazed blankly at her. Just before her confidence in us, and our pride in our performance ebbed irretrievably away, I found myself saying 'Could you mean – *Joseph's Yard*?' She could! Minutes later she left rejoicing, Charles Keeping's superb latest title clutched to her bosom.

The bookseller may know the title but not have it in stock at that moment. In this case, he should be prepared to take your order for it, and advise you when it is available. There is always the possibility that the title is out of print and therefore not obtainable, unless you are lucky enough to find a secondhand copy. This is worth trying and can, in most towns and cities, be accomplished by telephone. Most local classified directories or yellow pages list secondhand bookshops.

If you have any reason to suspect that the title *is* in print, regardless of the bookseller's statement that it is not, you might like to write direct to the publisher. All publishers are deeply interested in the public's attitude to their books, and find it hard to get enough feedback. You never know – your letter may even contribute to a decision to reprint.

Don't hesitate, even if you feel slightly self-conscious, to request details from either librarian or bookseller. Be polite and friendly, but firm. Both exist to give you service. You have a right to the information.

Be sure, also, to include your children in the 'finding out' game. They will quickly start using the terms themselves : 'copy', 'title', 'in stock', 'out of print'. Some years ago I was explaining to my family my inability to procure a particular brand of toothpaste. 'Must be out of print,' said our five-year-old!

Children feel more sure of themselves, less buffeted by fate and adults, if they are included. They will grow into adults who ask questions, if, as children, they come to expect answers. Bring them up to believe that finding out – about anything – is not only possible, but fun.

Why Books?

1
Why Books?

From the moment a baby first opens her eyes, she is learning. Sight, sound, and sensation together spark off a learning process which will continue to the end of her life, and determine in large measure the sort of person she will become.

Although the process is continuous, however, it is not even. At certain times learning will proceed at almost reckless pace; at others it will seem to have stopped, or at least to be in recess.

Scientists tell us that approximately one half of a person's ultimate intelligence is developed by the age of four, with another thirty per cent accruing by the age of eight. Clearly, what happens during these years matters.

In families where little thought is given to the need for early stimulation, it is quite common for parents to become concerned later about a child's poor progress at school. All too often, this leads to the negative reactions of urging, nagging, blaming ... usually to no avail. The days when the child's whole being radiated a joyful and receptive enthusiasm for learning have passed, unrecognized and little used.

Perhaps this sounds overdramatic. But it is true that the first three or four years are still seen by many people as a time when children are most tiresome, rather than as a period during which learning proceeds at almost breathtaking speed. Toddlers want constantly to touch things which may break, to attempt skills which are beyond them. They ask 'why?' and 'how?' repetitively and infuriatingly. They shout with rage when thwarted in their destructive purposes, and will not learn that this behaviour is anti-social and cannot be allowed. These are the constant complaints of some parents. Understandably, they want this stage to pass as quickly as possible.

But take heart! The same period may be seen in another way altogether. How about this?

'Early childhood is a time when children are at their most engaging, when the learning process may be seen with utmost clarity. They want to explore everything, discovering for themselves how things feel, how they work, how they sound when banged together, or dropped. They want to poke knobs and press switches and have a hand in everything. They naturally resent any attempt to curb this interesting experimentation, and protest in the only way they know, with vocally expressed rage.'

Which interpretation will *you* have?

I've long believed that a parent's only hope for real living (as against mere survival) during this period is to 'opt in'; to become personally involved in the youngster's learning life, so that triumphs and satisfactions, as well as defeats and reversals, feature daily. If you can believe that the latest atrocity is based on a desire to experiment, rather than to torture *you*, you'll feel better. You may be able to devise a harmless game which fulfils the same (apparently diabolical) purpose; but at least your dismay need not be coloured by the suspicion that you are raising a monster.

I well remember our consternation when a small son, still under two, discovered that objects could be prised off out-of-reach shelves with a toy spade, an umbrella, a broom. It was bad enough to have one's precious books crashing about; a heavy vase or a potted plant might have killed him. I don't recall any neat solution, but he was not our first child and we managed to avoid the worst excesses of parental outrage. We had learned real humility by the time this child turned into the very constructive and enterprising boy that was lurking beneath the two-year-old horror.

The other outstanding conclusion of scientists which relates to our present purpose is that language stands head and shoulders over all other tools as an instrument of learning. It takes only a little reflection to see that it is language that gives humankind its lead in intelligence over all other species. Only people are capable of abstract thought. Only people can stand back and contemplate their own situations. No other creatures can assemble, mentally, a list of ideas, consider them, draw conclusions and then explain their reasoning. Human beings can do this because they possess language; only the most rudimentary thought would be possible otherwise.

Just a little more reflection produces the conclusion that if thought depends upon language, then the quality of an individual's thought will depend upon the quality of that language. Language is, indeed, in the centre of the stage as far as learning and intelligence are concerned.

How *do* children learn to use language?

From their earliest days, unless they are deaf, babies will be listening to language. At the same time, they will be producing their own sounds, those familiar cooing and gurgling noises which are characteristic of all human babies. At other times of course, the noises they produce are strident and angry, making known their hunger, their discomfort, or their need for human contact. But always, from the beginning of life, the sounds babies produce are extensions of themselves. They are their way of expressing feeling, making known their needs to other human beings.

These early noises are, simultaneously, the raw material from which speech will be forged, and the first, instinctive attempt to communicate. Even at as early as a few weeks or a month, a baby will be soothed by a human voice uttering comforting words close by. This essentially emotional response provides early evidence of a truth which has emerged in the field of language study: feeling is an important component of language learning. A child learns to use language in interaction with other human beings, and this learning proceeds best against a background of affectionate feedback from the person who is closest to the child. This does not have to be the mother, but it does seem that a child's greatest hope of having her language needs totally and joyfully met in the first few years lies in the almost constant presence of one person who loves her, and wants to communicate with her. For it is through such caring, verbal interaction that the child learns best to use language.

At first, her attempt to name an object may be an approximation only. Her parent will accept her utterance with pleasure, often repeating it in correct form, or supplying the rest of the sentence which was so clearly implied.

> 'Ninner!'
> 'Yes, I know you are hungry and want your
> dinner.'

Long before she utters her first word, however, the child is involved in a two-way process which is steadily and surely building a foundation for her later performance in the language game. Constantly surrounded by language, she is building structures in her mind into which her speech, and later, reading, will fit. The form of these structures will depend on the amount and complexity of the speech she hears. The fortunate child in our society listens to articulate adults using language fluently. She will be accustomed to hearing ideas expressed and opinions defended. She will know, long before she can contribute herself, that relationships are forged through this two-way process of speaking and listening; that warmth and humour have a place in the process, as have all other human emotions.

It seems that language learning has a great deal to do with emotion and the development of relationships. This is seen to perfection in the interaction between parent and baby; eyes locked together, the adult almost physically drawing 'verbal' response from the baby, both engulfed by that unique experience of intimate and joyful 'connecting' which sets the pattern of relationship between two people.

For the baby, the experience is vital. It has long been believed that the tone of this first relationship carries over into all subsequent relationships, so that the child is equipped (or not) for successful emotional encounters. That language learning also gets its start, for better or worse, during this process, seems clear.

From this point there seems to be a circular process in operation which determines the direction which the child–parent relationship will take. Ideally, the baby's joyful response to the parent's approach sparks off delight and satisfaction in the adult, and ensures the continuation of the process. If the adult already uses language fluently, as a major tool of relationship, the baby's language development follows as the night the day. Surely, in every generation since the dawn of civilization, fortunate children and the adults who cared for them have demonstrated this truth.

Why, then, do we need to worry about it, or bother describing the process?

Because there is sadly irrefutable evidence that millions of the world's children have no chance at all of finding an adult partner in the early language game. And of these millions, a very large proportion are deprived by ignorance and the circumstances of their lives, rather than the absence of adults who care for them. All too often, language impoverishment is an established fact by the time a child starts school. And language is, undeniably, essential to learning. Tragedy has already entered the life of the five- or six-year-old whose early years have not provided him with the tools of learning.

It must be admitted that the ideas about using books that such a volume as this offers are inaccessible to many of these children and their parents. But this does not mean that these parents are uncaring. In my experience, the vast majority of parents of babies want to do the best they can for their children. Identifying 'the best', however, may be difficult, if not impossible.

Persuading such parents to read to their babies is not as unlikely an idea as it may seem at first. It is one which I offer constantly to the young mothers who make up the groups which I am asked to address. These are seldom 'educated' young women; more often, they are working-class wives, prey to all the modern ills of loneliness, boredom, strain and uncertainty which suburban life engenders.

It is difficult to persuade parents to read to nine-year-olds, or even six-year-olds, if the practice has not been established early. The children may resist, suspecting the adult's motive, or be unprepared to believe that the experience will be enjoyable. Many adults are keenly aware of their own shortcomings in the reading-aloud field. But babies are quite uncritical, and utterly accepting of adult attention; they provide a totally captive audience, accomplishing marvels in parental self-esteem. And practice does make perfect. The assured adult presenter of *Harry the Dirty Dog*, three years later, will have quite forgotten his fumbling performance on *b is for bear*, all those years ago!

It is my firm belief that giving the parent the idea of 'the book as a tool' will do more for the dual purpose of establishing the parent–child relationship and ensuring the child's adequate language development, than any amount of advice on *talking* to babies. None of us can endlessly initiate speech; we run out of ideas, or just plain get sick of it. The lives of babies and toddlers, even favoured ones, are limited. The experience just isn't there to provide the raw material for constant verbal interaction, without inevitable boredom on the child's part, and desperation on the adult's. But if books are added . . .

It is not possible to gauge the width and depth of the increase in a child's grasp of the world that comes with access to books. Contact with children of very tender years – two and three years of age – engenders a sense of awe at the way their understanding outruns their capacity for expression, the way their speech strains constantly to encompass their awareness, to represent reality as they see it. Shades of meaning which may be quite unavailable to the child of limited language experience are startlingly present in the understanding – and increasingly in the speech – of the 'well-read-to' toddler.

A small grandson, nearly twenty-three months old, preceded me up the stairs recently. Straining to hold the handrail, which he could hardly reach, he stumbled and recovered himself. 'Nearly fell,' he said. Then fearing that perhaps this failed to cover the situation exactly he added 'Almost!' This little boy looks like a two-year-old and certainly exhibits the full range of two-year-old characteristics (by turn, engaging and enraging). But his range of reference, his appreciation of degree, and in particular his consciousness of language and the way it *works* is impressive.

He lives with his parents in a very isolated area, several hundred miles away. When they arrived on holiday recently, he spoke beautifully, saying 'yes', whenever the affirmative was called for. Under the influence of the adolescents in the family, he converted 'yes' to 'yeah' in no time at all. At dinner one night someone mentioned this. Our two-year-old gave every sign of appreciating the difference and its significance. 'Not yess-ss!' he shouted, banging his spoon and laughing. 'Yeah!' He seemed to understand the general merriment in an uncannily mature way. Earlier he had corrected his mother when she referred by name to a character encountered for the first time in a new book that morning. 'Doctor *Crank*,' he said firmly, in response to her tentative 'Doctor Shanks?' Earlier still, in a department store, he had been whisked without preparation on to an escalator, a totally new experience. His dismay was fast turning to panic by the time his mother's reassurance came. 'Remember? Corduroy went on an escalator.' One could almost see his re-interpretation of the experience as familiar. If his good friend Corduroy could go on an escalator, so could Anthony!

In this family, mother and small son spend many hours alone together, in near-blizzard conditions for much of the year. Anthony's father is often away until the little boy is in bed, and company is difficult to provide. His mother's way of filling the long hours has always involved books. He has been read to constantly, as much for his parents' needs as his own, from birth.

At nearly two, he is the most 'experienced' toddler I know – and yet a huge proportion of this experience has been at second hand. His first visit to the zoo was a journey of rediscovery. 'Zebra!' 'Giraffe!' 'Lion!' Let no 'expert' persuade you that the small child should be introduced, in books, only to those objects which he has experienced in the flesh. Anthony has made joyful acquaintance with countless people, animals, objects and ideas, all between the covers of books, in his first two years of life, to his own incalculable advantage.

To strike one last, I hope conclusive blow for the introduction of books to pre-schoolers, let me establish the connection between early book-usage and later skills in reading.

It is useless to deny that there are, here and there, children who will have difficulty in learning to read despite having been surrounded by books from an early age. Such children probably have some 'specific learning difficulty' which may be impossible to diagnose except in the most general way. But they do have some rare but *real* disability.

For every such child, there are thousands whose reading failure seems unrelated to any specific handicap. They just can't read, at an age by which reading has usually been mastered. These are the children who are, almost inevitably, 'short' on language; short on concepts, on the 'patterns' of the tongue of their culture. Book language is an unfathomable mystery to them. It is a foreign language, not their own. I believe that these children need, more than anything else, a crash course in listening; to people who have something to say to them, and want to hear their ideas in return; to stories which will expand their view of the world; stories that will stir their emotions and quicken their curiosity. Then there may be some chance of these children reading for themselves – if caring good-humoured people will only guide them through the mechanics, and show them that most of what they need for reading they have already, in their own minds, and bodies, and hearts.

There is nothing magic about the way contact with books in early years produces early readers. One would surely expect it to. A baby is learning about the way language arises from the page each time her parent opens a book, from earliest days. She is linking the human voice to the print at a very early age. Given repeated opportunity, she notices how the adult attends to the black marks, how he can't go on reading if the page is turned too soon . . .

Skills come apparently unbidden as the toddler advances into three- and four-year-old independence. Print is friendly and familiar for this child. She is already unconsciously finding landmarks, noting regular features, predicting patterns . . .

Unbidden? Not a bit of it! This child has had her reading skills handed her on a golden platter.

Too Little to Look?

2

Too Little to Look?

I am the sister of him
And he is my brother,
But he is too little for us to
Talk to each other;
So every morning I show him
My doll and my book,
But every morning he still is
Too little to look.

Ideally, a small pile of good books awaits the new baby's arrival. Friends and relations often request suggestions for presents, and gift money can be earmarked for books. In my family, we have a habit of sending a book for the 'displaced' baby. *Mr Gumpy's Outing*, 'For Jane, and Timothy when he is old enough,' is of much more use in a delicate family situation than a pair of bootees!

Keep the baby's books within reach, and make a practice of showing them to her from the day you first bring her home. The covers will be brightly illustrated, and at first you can encourage her to focus her eyes on these pictures. You can teach your baby a lot about books in the first few months.

To begin with, she will learn that a book is a thing, with different qualities from all other things. For many babies, the world must flow past in a succession of half-perceived images. Until their own physical development enables them to lift and turn their heads and focus their eyes, they must rely on obliging adults to help.

As early in her life as possible, start showing your baby successive pages of a suitable book. If you don't believe that this is making a start on her learning life, at least you'll believe that for both of you it is an agreeable way of spending time. Babies love to be held, and you will be getting your hand in early.

You will need books which have clearly defined, uncluttered pictures, in bright primary colours. The work of a Dutchman, Dick Bruna, is worth knowing about. Bruna books are simplicity itself. An apple, in *b is for bear*, is a bright red sphere, slightly indented where a green stalk is attached. The whole is outlined in black on a white page. I have yet to meet a very young baby who is not arrested by Bruna's apple.

Give her time to soak it up, meanwhile pointing to the black 'a' on the opposite page and saying anything that comes to mind; 'a is for apple' to start with, then any other cheerful and relevant comment. 'Look at the big, red apple.' Don't worry, when you come to successive pages, that she may never see a real live Eskimo or that castles are remote from her experience; 'e is for Eskimo' and 'c for castle' will be accepted in good faith, and their representations savoured. Other 'first' Bruna's are listed in the relevant section at the end of the chapter. Not all titles are suitable for the earliest listener, and the standard varies considerably.

At this very early stage, before babies can snatch and grab, you can safely use any book of your choice for read-aloud sessions. Before long, however, you will probably find yourself involved in a wrestling match unless you develop defensive tactics.

Some parents feel that a retreat to undamageable 'board' books is the only possible solution, but I feel that a compromise is possible. Later in this chapter I have touched on this subject in a paragraph on the physical handling of read-aloud sessions (see page 18).

The last few years have seen an explosion in the production of 'board' books. To augment the traditional article have come examples which are toys rather than books. In every conceivable shape and size, many of them make delightful and ornamental gifts, but need hardly concern us here. They tend to disappear as they are supplanted by even more original or outlandish varieties. Meanwhile the traditional book form endures.

I believe that certain criteria should be used in choosing board books, and that these are often overlooked. This, of course, does not really matter if the book is well produced and you want to try it, but it is sensible to apportion family 'book' money with an eye to maximum benefit, and the crucial question to ask is: 'Will this book stand repeated readings?'

Here are my suggestions.

First, board books should be provided only for true babies – and then only as an addition to a collection, never as the sole source of read-aloud material. By the time children are eighteen months old they need a much wider range of style, subject-matter and art form that can ever be supplied by board books; and surely, parents have their rights, too!

Next, I have never given a child a board book which has no text. This is a personal preference, certainly, and one you may happily ignore, if you *like* talking about pictures. (There's nothing to stop you doing this anyway – and I am happy with a single letter, as in Bruna's non-board *b is for bear*.) Believing as I do, however, that babies are attending to print, noting its shape – what one might call its 'conventions' – from the time they are first given the chance to do so, I feel that this exposure may as well begin at birth.

My next rule of thumb: given that board books are for babies only, they should not explore themes which are not babyish. (A recently seen example shows a child of three or four lost in a supermarket: a relevant topic, with imaginative potential. Why not ensure that the story reaches its appropriate audience? It seems unlikely to do so in a babies' board-book series.)

To conclude: as board books will be used often by babies without parental supervision, they should be brightly coloured, and use an art style which is clear and uncluttered. It should hardly need stating that they should be strongly bound, with pages which will resist the attempts at demolition that will surely be their lot. Above all, they must not grow soggy when sucked!

An occasional parent – or, more usually, grandparent – asks about 'old-fashioned rag books'. These seem, mercifully, to have died a decent death. I never felt that rag books *were* books. Books are made of paper which, in all its various forms, none the less looks, feels, smells and behaves like paper. Rag books, as I recall them, looked, felt and behaved like limp dish-rags – and before long smelt like dirty dish-rags. I cannot regret their passing. I don't believe that babies were ever deluded into regarding them as books, anyway – and the near glut of wipeable board books certainly renders them redundant in these hygiene-conscious times. A recent addition to the baby book scene is a type of spongy-to-touch, brightly coloured little volume which can even be taken into the bath. Methuen publishes two series, each featuring the work of an artist who is already famous in the field. There are four 'Soft Spots' by Eric Hill, who has also produced the Little Spot Board Books described below. The famous Dutch artist, Dick Bruna, is responsible for four Bruna Baby Books in the same tradition; and these resilient little plastic books behave like books.

An outstanding example of the board-book category has been devised and illustrated by Simms Taback, and published by Heinemann. Called 'Word Books for Babies', there are four titles: Clothing, Playthings, Food and Animals. Each page reveals a brightly outlined object against a clear background, with a single word in lower case letters: sheep, pig, elephant, zebra . . . Each is tiny, tough and true to its own nature.

Mog and Me and Mog's Family of Cats present the inestimable Mog (see Book List 4, page 119) in board form, suitably underplayed for the very young. Judith Kerr manages a text which is brief but never boring: a bonus for deserving parents. 'I have to get dressed, but Mog wears her fur all the time.' These are square, satisfying little volumes which will appeal to children and adults alike.

Helen Oxenbury's 'Baby Board books' – and the second series, somewhat bafflingly entitled just 'Board Books', but retaining the same size, format and level – are utterly engaging little books which will have parents chuckling from first opening to last. Depicted are babies, divested of the prettiness often accorded them by unobservant adults, but accorded that diabolical innocence in the face of which parental or other grown-up ammunition is powerless. (An all-too-familiar quality to those who actually live with babies.) The pictures themselves are so clear, so uncluttered, the situations so recognizable, that we need not feel guilty about the books' appeal to ourselves, for children love them too. Here is true sharing of that 'slice of life' which constitutes a good book.

As I write this, I have just been shown proof pages of a new 'Big Board Book' by Helen Oxenbury – one of a series of four, I'm told – called *Clap Hands*. Middle-sized and squarish, this is, so the catalogue tells me, a 'multi-ethnic' board book; and certainly, the first double spread shows babies in two shades of brown, one in yellow and another in pink, all in exuberant, if somewhat staggery celebration of the text: 'Clap hands, dance and spin . . .' This is followed by four more, just as delectable double spreads: 'open wide and pop it in, blow a trumpet, bang a drum, wave to Daddy, wave to Mum.'

The addition of a text pleases me, and the vibrant tone of both colour and theme will please everyone. All four titles will serve through the second year too – but start collecting them now. The others are *Tickle Tickle*, *Say Good Night* and *All Fall Down*. Two other equally useful and attractive series will be found in the list at the end of the chapter.

Before I leave the subject of board books I should perhaps point out an obvious fact: babies themselves, much less concerned with endurability than their parents, cannot be expected to prefer board books to the true variety, if exposed to both. At six months, my granddaughter Bridget reserved her greatest enthusiasm for *Teddybears 1 to 10* and *Home Sweet Home*. Six months later, both books are grubby, much mended – and still deeply loved. Would she have liked them as well in board form? There is no way of knowing.

To return to the world of 'real' books – in all their rustly, crinkly, delectable vulnerability!

Alphabet books seem to be particularly useful at this stage, probably because so many of them are very simple. Brian Wildsmith's *ABC* is a feast of rich colour, a delight for any age. It has become, deservedly, a modern classic. John Burningham's *ABC* will be favoured by some parents, and is loved in my own family. Burningham's king and queen are masterly and majestic; and the sooner babies start making the acquaintance of the monarchs of fiction, in word and in picture, the better. There is a spirited pair in Rodney Peppé's *The Alphabet Book*. Each double spread in this excellent A B C covers two successive letters; a single line of simple text at the bottom of the page accentuates the appropriate letter, which is both larger and more heavily printed than the others.

> This is the **a**nchor . . . that holds the **b**oat.
> Here is a **c**upboard. Count the **d**olls,

(which are revealed sitting in three engaging rows, once the cupboard is opened).

Start *now*, running your finger casually under the text as you say it. Not always, but occasionally. By the time your baby is old enough to connect the black marks on the page with your voice, the knowledge that the meaning arises from the writing will have lodged in her bones. Peppé's illustrations are particularly suited to the very young child's need for clarity, colour, and no-clutter. *The Alphabet Book* is a totally satisfying experience, with its square, stiffish pages, and striking pictures. It is out of print at the moment, but your library should be able to help.

Helen Oxenbury's A B C of Things, a tall, narrow book which offers a number of 'things' connected in cheerful, nonsensical fashion, is transformed by this artist's unique and humorous drawings into a masterpiece. Her *Numbers of Things* is equally satisfying.

'Number' and 'colour' books seem made for the under-ones, too, and remember that these, like alphabet books, all come into their own again once the child is learning to read, to count, and to recognize colours.

There can be no artist working in the field at present whose style speaks more directly to the very young than Emilie Boon. Clear outline, bright but not garish colour and an overall quality of warmth without sentimentality produce pictures which are instantly received as exactly right, one suspects, by the youngest viewer. *1 2 3, How Many Animals Can you See?* is an excellent example. Each left-hand page presents a simple sentence using the appropriate number in word form:

> *Duck paddles up,*
> *That makes three.*

Below, a large clear numeral in bright colour takes the eye with its clarity. Opposite, the named animal joins the existing band, its members making their jaunty way through a landscape which offers points of focus without any clutter. Altogether a buoyant book, which will retain the child's interest for several years.

Jan Pieńkowski as an artist has many moods, but nowhere has he more clearly met a real need than in a set of small books covering such topics as colour, size, number and the alphabet: twelve titles in all. Several of these – notably *Colours* and *Sizes* – are probably more useful than the others at this stage, though all arrest the baby's eye with that same brilliance and clarity which also characterizes Bruna's work. Their size (17 cm × 17 cm) is important too; for attention-getting, a small, easily manipulated book is best.

There is another useful category which my family calls 'noise' books. These are loved by very small children, not least because they demand adult performance.

Trouble in the Ark, by Gerald Rose, though ostensibly an 'early reader', is also an excellent 'noise' book. It begins with the animals crowded together in the ark. A fly starts the trouble; 'he *buzzed* at mouse, who *squeaked* at rabbit, who *squealed* at rhinoceros ...' Inevitably, wolf howls, hen cackles, lion roars ... until 'just then dove flew in with an olive twig', at which stage Noah himself adds to the rumpus with a 'Yahoo!' and 'Yippee!' which can be relied upon to delight the young, accompanied as it inevitably will be with wild bouncing-on-parental-knee! Here is language which is rich, action which is headlong, and humour which is compelling. Vigorous, clear and colourful pictures of each animal annoying his neighbour render the whole a joy.

Peter Spier has produced serveral 'noise' books, each astonishingly comprehensive in its field. I remember emerging from a prolonged and enforced performance of *Gobble, Growl, Grunt* with racked vocal cords and ruined throat while on holiday with several grandchildren some years ago. The tyrant of the piece was a grandson of two-and-a-half whose enthusiasm for this book knew no bounds. His sister, aged six, disapproved strongly of it. 'It's not a real story at all,' she declared firmly, and I agreed. But I was no match for her brother. No one else offered to perform, and I weakly continued. (The children's parents pointed out with some justification that I had given it to him for Christmas. They also contrived to leave it behind when they left a few days before we did!)

'Noise' books are almost, but not quite, gimmicky; but they are fun, and may be used with babies long before their 'point' is understood.

This is probably the place to insert a few hints about the physical management of read-aloud sessions.

The baby is, as mentioned earlier, totally captive only while he is still unable to use his arms and hands for batting and snatching. Thereafter, you will have to find some course which is acceptable to both of you; that will neither totally frustrate him, nor so thwart *your* purpose that you give up.

To begin with, you must accept that any baby worth his salt *will* want to grab the book as soon as his physical development renders this possible. This does not mean that he is not interested; on the contrary, he is *so* interested that he wants to experience that delectable object (the book) in the way he likes best of all. He wants to grab it and cram it into his mouth. (If you find this kind of reaction too exasperating, try to imagine what it's like to be a parent whose baby, for some tragic reason, cannot use his hands to grab anything.)

Your best course of action is to play for time. If you can arrange for him to experience real visual and aural satisfaction from contact with books, you may find that he modifies his snatching behaviour at a surprisingly early age. Be sure to give him a rattle or similar toy to suck while listening and watching, and remember that, even at this early stage, a dramatic performance, with actions and changes of voice tone, will be more entertaining than a monotonous one.

Many of the books suggested in this chapter have been written for young children, rather than babies. This reflects my own preference, rather than any lack of very simple books – and certainly relates to my own habit of reading aloud to babies, established long before the appearance of special 'baby' books. Over the last decade publishers have responded to an upsurge of interest in very early education by an increasing flow of such books. While I applaud this trend, I still insist that any book *you* happen to like will serve as well; it is your involvement with your baby that matters most. And why worry if the characters in your baby's books are operating at a level she will not reach for several years? This is true of the people around her, who walk, talk, and conduct their lives in complex ways before her sponge-like contemplation. How much could she possibly learn from the boring company of other babies?

Babies need people: talking, laughing, warm-hearted people, constantly drawing them into their lives, and offering them the world for a playground. Let's give them books to parallel this experience; books where language and illustration activate the senses, so that meaning slips in smoothly, in the wake of feeling.

For your own sake, read aloud an interesting, lively story from time to time. Endless improvisation on the near-textless page can be tiring and boring. One of my daughters read *The Elephant and the Bad Baby* which is, strictly speaking, suitable for older children, to her small son, frequently, from five months, as this book was available and she enjoyed it herself. Shortly afterwards, *The Very Hungry Caterpillar* was introduced for the same reason, a varied selection of any-age picture books following soon after. This young mother mentioned a point that hadn't occurred to me in this connection: it is possible to feel quite self-conscious, carrying on an endless one-way conversation with a very young baby, whereas reading aloud is a *performance*. And to this performance, as to any other, you can bring spirit and individuality. Don't hesitate to move in time to the rhythm, to accentuate rhymes, to tickle or cuddle the baby at appropriate points (which she will come to anticipate), to turn over the page with a flourish . . . in short, to perform with style.

Your reward will come with your baby's response. You'll be astonished at how early she gives signs of knowing that, any minute now, the image will change. As your hand moves towards the top right-hand corner of the page, the baby's eyes will brighten. A flick – and a totally new vista is presented for her delight. You are staying in touch with her in the best possible way, if you can share her pleasure.

And please – please! – don't give up because your baby snatches at the book and appears to want only to eat it or throw it away. Cancelling the whole programme in the face of a few setbacks is like deciding to keep your child well away from the water until she can swim. There is ample evidence that three- and four-year-olds who meet books for the first time in their lives are inattentive and destructive. Your baby can put this stage behind her in the very early days, if you are patient. A little and often, is the rule of thumb.

A common mistake on the part of new parents is the assumption that for young children photographs of objects and scenes are preferable to drawings, paintings, or other art forms. This is seldom true.

Have you ever wondered why botany textbooks – or seamen's manuals – use *drawings* of plants and ships rather than photographs to illustrate their points? This is because an artist can include the features he needs for his purpose, and just as importantly, exclude those features which would distract the human eye, or mar the clarity of the intended impression. It is essential, in a serious textbook, that the shape, outline and detail of the represented object be shown in a way which permits no mistake. Thus, the author arranges for drawings, not photographs, to illustrate his points.

If students and adults find pictures simpler to follow than photographs, surely one would expect the young child to show similar preference? The three-dimensional quality of a photograph is a complication to a small child. There is a feeling abroad that it is important that small children recognize and name objects in their books. Even in this connection, flat representations win out.

And now to nursery rhymes.

Don't even consider facing parenthood without a really good collection. We all think we can remember them, but how many can we call to mind, offhand? Modern teachers tell us that many children come to school without knowing any.

You may ask 'Of what value are nursery rhymes in today's world?'

To begin with, nursery rhymes are part of our children's heritage, in an age when too little is handed down. There is a world of security and satisfaction in knowing that children don't really change from generation to generation; that some of the best things are still the oldest. We feel part of a great human progression as we see our children swept into the dance as we were before them. We convey our own deep satisfaction in this process, and rejoice in our children's in return.

And the rhymes themselves? Many of them began as political jingles concocted by adults, but over the years the children have taken them for their own. They have been polished and shone and their corners smoothed, until their form is, in many cases, perfect. If children are to love poetry later, they need to discover early the peculiar satisfaction which comes from experiencing form in language. This is not something which can ever be taught; how can a sensation be taught? But it will be there, in their repertoire of response, if it has been kindled in babyhood.

You may have to take this assertion on trust, if poetry has meant little to you in your own life. You may even doubt that it matters anyway, and this doubt is understandable. Fortunately you can relax, and use nursery rhymes and other poems with your baby without examining their long-term effects at all. The evidence will be undeniable that the baby loves them *now*. They are a real aid when you and your child are obliged to make the best of one another's company (as when you are driving and he is strapped into his car seat) or when you find yourself temporarily stranded without a book. You will certainly notice the way the rhymes bubble out of him once they are entrenched. You can hear the way his flow of language is improved with this constant repetition, see the way he moves joyfully to the rhythm, sense the satisfaction he feels in the rhyme. Patterns are being laid down here; patterns into which every sort of later literary and musical experience will fit.

You may still feel that some of the nursery rhymes are too nonsensical for modern use. In this workaday world, shouldn't our children be hearing only good sense?

Not a bit of it! An element of lunacy has always been cherished by children, and words which are not completely rational, but which offer an experience to the senses rather than the mind, help them towards a feeling for language itself, in all its diverse trappings. We are surely hoping to raise imaginative children, children who tap all the available resources, without and within? At all events, over-seriousness has no place in childhood.

The nursery rhyme edition you choose matters less than your own willingness to perform. It is better to have no book at all, if you are confident about your off-the-cuff talent, than to invest in an expensive volume and leave it on the shelf. The essential factor is your determination to surround your child with the jingles and rhymes of his culture; to invite his response to rhythm and rhyme, to gladden his heart and enliven his imagination.

The Mother Goose Treasury by Raymond Briggs is unlikely to be surpassed as a comprehensive, popular collection. The illustrations achieve a superb compromise between the 'traditional' (which is usually Victorian) and the modern, and have a clarity and robust vigour which appeal to child and adult alike. You may prefer the meticulous dignity and quiet colour of Kathleen Lines's *Lavender's Blue*, or the lavish purples and scarlets of Brian Wildsmith's *Mother Goose*. Your baby won't protest, so you may as well buy with your own pleasure in mind. You'll be more likely to use the book if you love it, and this is what matters.

Tomie de Paola's Mother Goose has now joined the ranks of these outstanding books, and sits very comfortably beside them; like *Lavender's Blue* and the collections of Briggs and Wildsmith, de Paola's book has a distinct and individual character and charm. There is both elegance and sensitivity in this artist's work. His pinks, blues and greens are soft and yet luminous, his line strong, his sense of design impeccable. Those who demand dignity and grace in their nursery rhymes need look no further.

Quite different, but notable in its own way is Michael Hague's *Mother Goose*. The illustrations are in the tradition of nineteenth-century artist Arthur Rackham, and do seem particularly well suited to the nursery rhyme world. Michael Hague's rather sombre reds, browns, blues and purples combine to produce strangely glowing pictures; his Jack and Jill double spread is unbeaten, to my taste, in its presentation of this universal rhyme. The forty-seven rhymes chosen include all the popular favourites and a sprinkling of less-known jingles. The text is clear and well placed, the book itself easier to handle than many collections.

Of course, you can swing to any extreme, in this fascinating field; the material is there for your choosing. *Rub-a-dub-dub* stretches to two soft-covered but stoutly built volumes, called severally *Nursery Rhymes* and *More Nursery Rhymes*. Both almost assault the eye with bright primary colour. Most openings have either plain, striped or polka-dotted borders in brilliant blues, reds and yellows. The style is that of the cartoonist. All characters are animals, real or bizarrely imagined; the overall tone is one of exaggeration and riotous action. All good fun, and certain to rivet the attention, if not cultivate the senses, of the young. (The blurb refers to a television tie-in, which is easy to imagine!)

You may search out any of these established versions, or find one of your own. It may even seem (and be) good sense to start with a cheap, mass-market version, or a paperback, while you make up your mind – or until Grandma resolves the matter by producing one that you hadn't encountered in your browsing.

I have heard a parent say, when shown one of the 'big' collections of nursery rhymes, 'It seems such a big book for such a little child,' and I understand this feeling. Briggs's *Treasury* certainly has to be supported by table, floor, or bed while being read, and a small child could hardly carry it safely.

Ideally, the collection of one's choice should be kept on table or shelf, and produced for shared sessions until the child is old enough to handle the book alone. You need not feel that these supervised sessions are repressive if the toddler has several small, cheap editions of his own – perhaps a Little Golden Book collection, and one or two of the small books by Allen Atkinson mentioned in the book list.

A natural extension of the nursery rhyme collection is the song book, complete with music. If you can play the piano, and have one in your home, your children will be especially lucky; but supplying such a book is a good idea, anyway. Most of us are familiar with the tunes for 'Jack and Jill,' 'Three Blind Mice' and 'The Farmer in the Dell' and learning that the little black dots and handles on the five-barred fence tell your voice where to go will do the baby no harm. You will almost certainly have a relation or friend who can demonstrate – perhaps on a guitar or recorder if no piano is available – with subsequent increase of interest in this different and fascinating book.

Sing Hey diddle diddle is an outstanding song book for home or school use. Containing '66 nursery rhymes with their traditional tunes', it will give years of enjoyable wear. The spiral binding allows the book to lie or sit flat for easy reference and its energetic, arresting pictures invite a small child to use it also as a picture book. Tunes are learnt easily, at this stage. Lack of an instrument need be no handicap if parents will perform vocally, however unskilled they feel. Audio tapes, easy to obtain and inexpensive, constitute an excellent source of tunes which, once learned, can be used with any book, or alone.

Songs, of course, are for any and all age groups, as long as they are lyrical and uncomplicated. *The Great Song Book* by Timothy John ranges from nursery rhymes through folk songs to lullabies and carols and has an extra bonus in its addition of guitar chords to the simple settings. This whole-of-life book is unfortunately out of print at present, but you may be able to find a secondhand copy. Tomi Ungerer's superbly set illustrations and the sturdy, manageable nature of the book itself make *The Great Song Book* especially valuable.

This may be a good time to state a belief I hold about duplication in books for the young. Far from rejecting a rhyme or poetry book (or later, a story collection) because it contains material available in already-owned titles, try to make sure that this repetition does occur. The child whose own familiar Humpty Dumpty resides between the covers of Briggs's *Treasury* will greet his prototype in other collections with cries of joyful recognition. This is an essentially human reaction; we all have it. If the version is slightly different, read it as presented. The sooner small children become interested in the fascinating tendency of rhyme and story to vary from time to time and place to place, the better. Of course no one parent could afford to buy five or six editions to facilitate this process, but perhaps the major family collection of nursery rhymes could be augmented – and given new life – by one of these shorter gems? If you add library borrowing, reciprocal arrangements with friends and the odd paperback, you could raise a connoisseur!

It is hard to draw the line between nursery rhymes and what I call 'jingles'. Where, in your classification, do 'This Little Pig went to Market . . .' and 'Frère Jacques . . .' belong? No need to decide. Several thoroughly competent editors have taken the matter into their own hands and provided staple editions which ensure that the field is covered.

This Little Puffin, compiled by Elizabeth Matterson, should be provided as a matter of course. Fortunately, this is now available in hardback – it is easy to wear out several copies of the paperback edition. It describes itself as 'a remarkable treasury of finger plays and singing and action games . . .' and goes on to prove this claim incontestably.

Round and Round the Garden, compiled by Sarah Williams has everything: forty thoroughly usable rhymes, instructions for adults which are pictured as well as described, and illustrations by Ian Beck which are clear, colourful and expressive. The same author and artist have combined to produce *Ride a Cock-Horse* which, divided into sections entitled 'Knee-Jogging Rhymes', 'Bouncing and Dancing Rhymes', Patting and Clapping Rhymes', and 'Lullaby and Rocking Rhymes', provides a wealth of material for parents and willing friends and relations.

Ownership of one or more of these splendid books will increase your confidence in the field. But private rehearsals will be necessary if you are to manage baby and book together. And remember that mastering both rhyme and action ahead of time is the ideal in the case of finger plays and rhymes requiring physical performance. The book can be used for reference and for reading, but is best cast aside for energetic action games. Fortunately, most babies prefer one single action rhyme performed a dozen times to twelve separate offerings, so you need not feel pushed. And each book gives explicit directions, telling you not only which rhymes and jingles to use with your baby, but, in detail, how to handle him, tickle, pat, rock and jog him, enlivening the performance with the words. The

jingle is the pudding and the actions are the sauce, or vice
versa . . .

You will find that you sing some of the rhymes, always, and say
others. Respond in your own individual way to jingles; follow the
suggestions given for actions if you wish, or invent your own.
Before long, rhymes will come unbidden, to accompany the mundane round of life. Your baby's days will be enriched, and your
task lightened.

Human response to touch and sound gets its start here. Too
many of our children grow up lacking the capacity to use *all* their
senses, physical, emotional and intellectual. 'It is the world's one
crime its babes grow dull . . . ,' said the poet Vachel Lindsay nearly
fifty years ago. We have done little to negate this charge since
then.

Make sure that both you and your child emerge from the years
of babyhood with all the old rhymes tucked safely away, as familiar
as nappies and teddybears, and just as essential. You will both be
well armed for the years ahead.

Book List 1
Books to Use in the First Year

The titles listed here are suitable for introduction in the first year of a baby's life, but will be in use for years. For ease of reference, titles have been grouped in categories.

Those titles which are mentioned in the previous chapter are marked with an asterisk (*). The name of the hardback publisher is given first in the brackets, followed by that of the paperback publisher, where there is one.

Please use this list in conjunction with the one at the end of the next chapter. There is a great deal of overlap between all the lists.

ALPHABET BOOKS

*ABC John Burningham (Cape)
*ABC Brian Wildsmith (Oxford)
* The Alphabet Book Rodney Peppé (Viking Kestrel)
*b is for bear Dick Bruna (Methuen)
*Helen Oxenbury's ABC of Things Helen Oxenbury (Heinemann/ Picture Lions paperback)

NUMBER AND COUNTING BOOKS

I can count Dick Bruna (Methuen)
Brilliant slabs of primary colour in the tradition established by b is for bear. Small, comfortable format makes this, with the next title, a real 'first' book.

Numbers   Jan Pieńkowski   (Heinemann/Puffin paperback)
**Numbers of Things*   Helen Oxenbury   (Heinemann/Picture Lions paperback)
One Bear All Alone   Caroline Bucknall   (Macmillan)
This sure-footed book will be enjoyed for years, once acquired. Its simple couplets are easily and quickly read aloud, and its agreeable, graphic pictures faithfully depict the action: factors which make it especially suitable for first-year use. From

> *One bear all alone,*
> *Sitting by the telephone*

to

> *Ten tired bears have gone to bed.*
> *Can you count each sleepy head?*

the growing group is revealed in all its furry and lovable bearness. This author-artist has avoided over-cleverness and yet produced a book which adult, as well as child, will find both endearing and funny.
**1 2 3 How Many Animals Can You See?*   Emilie Boon   (Orchard Books)

BOARD BOOKS

*'*Baby Board Books*'
*'*Big Board Books*'
*'*Board Books*'   all by Helen Oxenbury   (Walker)
*'*Bruna Baby Books*' (4 titles)   Dick Bruna   (Methuen)
At the Zoo
On the Farm
All My Toys
Here's Miffy
*'Little Spot Board Books' (6 titles)   Eric Hill   (Heinemann)
These satisfying little books feature the same irresistible puppy whose activities, as depicted in the 'flap' books described in Chapter 3, have become everyday fare for many millions of the

world's young. The format is small, the pictures bright and uncluttered. The books are themselves shaped, to encourage small fingers to explore.

Mog and Me

Mog's Family of Cats both by Judith Kerr   (Collins)

'My Big Little Fat Books'   Ann Ricketts   (Brimax)

There are four titles in this series, the rather simpering title of which gives no clue to its quality. The books concern themselves, in turn, with numbers, toys, animals and sound; and each is splendid in its own way. Exceptionally clear, pastel-tinted pages present one object and one bold line of print, in three of the titles. *Look and Listen* – a 'noise' book actually – has two lines of text, one over and one under the picture, but these are brief in the extreme, each lower line being devoted to the noise made by the animal or object depicted. 'Look at the dog . . . woof woof woof. Look at the bells . . . jingle jingle jingle.' Of their kind, these are superlative books.

*'Soft Spots' (4 titles)   Eric Hill   (Methuen)

Spot Goes Splash!

Spot's Toys

Spot's Friends

Sweet Dreams, Spot!

*'Word Books for Babies' (4 titles)   Simms Taback   (Heinemann)

NOISEBOOKS

Gobble, Growl, Grunt   Peter Spier   (World's Work)

Old MacDonald had a Farm   William Stobbs   (Oxford)

This is the old rhyme, which may as well be mastered by the parents of babies in their first year; it will crop up at many points during childhood. (See Book List 4, page 120, for a 'flap' version.) This well-established artist has enjoyed himself here, producing expansive spreads of astonishing brilliance and complexity, which are never jumbled. Mercifully, in this version, one is not invited to include every animal already mentioned

every time another is introduced, although this exhausting formula is provided for the hardy on the endpapers, along with
music. Babies will love the quacking and oinking – and later
pore over the pages.

* *Trouble in the Ark*   Gerald Rose   (Bodley Head/Magnet paperback)

NURSERY RHYMES

The Helen Oxenbury Nursery Rhyme Book   Brian Alderson, illus.
Helen Oxenbury   (Heinemann)

This handsome volume would make a wonderful present for a
second, or subsequent baby; the omission of many favourites
rules it out as a family's only *Mother Goose*, I believe. However,
its complement of less-known but attractive rhymes gives it an
individual charm – and Helen Oxenbury's illustrations have a
balanced elegance which is still robust.

* *Lavender's Blue*   Kathleen Lines, illus. Harold Jones   (Oxford)
* *Mother Goose*   Michael Hague   (Methuen)
* *Mother Goose*   Brian Wildsmith   (Oxford)
Mother Goose's Nursery Rhymes   illus. Allen Atkinson   (Bantam
Books)

There are four strongly bound soft-covered little books in this
useful set, with names like *Little Boy Blue and Other Favourites*.
The covers, each with enchanting illustration framed in a lilac
border, catch the eye immediately, and the contents do not
disappoint. The rhymes include a wide selection of well- and
lesser-known examples, and there is just enough on each page to
read before little hands turn the page. I would buy all four and
keep them in separate 'emergency' locations – the car and the
shopping bag, for example.

* *The Mother Goose Treasury*   Raymond Briggs   (Hamish Ham-
ilton/Puffin paperback)
Nicola Bayley's Book of Nursery Rhymes   Nicola Bayley   (Cape/
Puffin paperback)

This book has the air of a collection of prints; I have yet to meet an adult who is not simultaneously astonished and enchanted by it. The hard-covered version is perfect for holding in one hand and reading aloud, but its almost indescribable beauty may make you reluctant to risk impetuous little fingers. The paperback version may suffice; but the original book is incomparable.

Over the Moon: A Book of Nursery Rhymes Charlotte Voake (Walker)

A book of satisfying shape and size, in many ways easier to handle, and yet just as comprehensive as most of the 'big' collections. This is a well-balanced book. Charlotte Voake's delicate watercolour paintings have spirit, grace and humour, and her black-and-white line illustrations provide variety. There is something to be said for not having too many rhymes on each page; a feature which may well make this collection a favourite.

Rub-a-dub-dub: Nursery Rhymes Alan Rogers (Granada/ Granada paperback)

Rub-a-Dub-Dub: More Nursery Rhymes Alan Rogers (Granada/ Granada paperback)

Tomie de Paola's Mother Goose Tomie de Paola (Methuen)

SONGBOOKS

Sing Hey diddle diddle Beatrice Harrop (ed.), illus. Frank Francis and Bernard Cheese (A. & C. Black)

The Faber Book of Nursery Songs D. Mitchell & C. Blyton, illus. Alan Howard (Faber)

A sturdy, established collection of simple songs in simple settings. Black-and-white illustrations (on most pages) are spirited, and the coloured, whole-page pictures a delight.

The Great Song Book Timothy John, illus. Tomi Ungerer (A. & C. Black)

JINGLES, ACTION RHYMES AND FINGER PLAYS

Ride a Cock-Horse
Round and Round the Garden both by Sarah Williams, illus. Ian Beck   (Oxford/Oxford paperback)
This Little Puffin ...   Elizabeth Matterson   (Viking Kestrel/ Puffin paperback)

INDIVIDUAL TITLES

Baby Boo!   Colin and Jacqui Hawkins   (Pepper Press)
  A roly-poly teddybear raises a plump arm in front of his face in the time-honoured 'Boo!' tradition on the cover of this delectable book. Two flaps per double spread – a total of fourteen flaps in all – open to reveal a succession of animal, human or toy characters, all of whom shout 'Boo!' in answer to a simple rhyming question: 'Munch, munch, who's having lunch?' Appropriate or unexpected, they are all hearty, easily identified and expressively depicted. Astonishing clarity had been achieved by the use of brilliant colour against a white background. An outstanding book.
Brown Bear, Brown Bear, What Do You See?   Bill Martin Jr, illus. Eric Carle   (Hamish Hamilton/Picture Lions paperback)
  I recall finding a tiny version of this outstanding book in an American 'Reader' series fourteen years ago, and recognizing its potential immediately. Subsequent use with my granddaughter Cushla confirmed my opinion – and when, recently, Hamish Hamilton published a large, handsome version in England, I cheered. Here's what I said in *Cushla and Her Books*: 'This book uses a repetitive device to tie together, in rhymed couplets, a list of likely and unlikely animals – a black sheep, a blue horse, a purple cat:

> Brown bear, brown bear, what do you see?
> I see a yellow duck looking at me.
> Yellow duck, yellow duck, what do you see? . . .

It seems likely that from Cushla's point of view *Brown Bear* had everything. It embodied the clear, bright no-background illustrations of the Bruna books and the repetitive jaunty rhyme of The House that Jack Built. At all events, it slid easily into favour at this time.' As it will today, for any first- or second-year baby lucky enough to encounter it.

*Colours

*Sizes both by Jan Piénkowski   (Heinemann/Puffin paperback)

Henry's Busy Day   Rod Campbell   (Viking Kestrel)

The pages in this sure-footed book for the very young are stiff enough to qualify it for board-book status. Henry is a rumbustious puppy whose escapades, recorded in no more than six to eight words on nine successive double spreads (with speech balloons supporting, tersely), are predictable: he digs holes, chews slippers, and chases pigeons. On the last page we see Henry asleep in his basket exhausted. Stroking his 'real' woolly coat is an unexpected bonus at this point – though Henry is a dog to be enjoyed, through all his innocent antics.

A companion volume, *Misty's Mischief*, presents the family cat (at whom Henry barks in *his* book) in centre stage, with *her* misdemeanours catalogued and described – and her sleek grey fur is available for stroking on the last page. Satisfying stuff, in your first year of life, when cats and dogs, way down there with you, are fascinating to contemplate.

Home Sweet Home   Maureen Roffey   (Bodley Head/Piccolo paperback)

'Does a cat live in a kennel?' asks the cat on the first page in this striking book; and indeed, the bright green kennel on the opposite page reveals, through its door (which is a real hole in the stiffish page), part of a furry animal. Turn over and 'No!' we are told. 'A dog lives in a kennel, of course.' Now we are *inside* the kennel with the big furry dog, while the cat peers through the door. And so on, to the end. Our one-year-old Bridget's copy, from which I am quoting, is so adorned with sticky mending tape and the evidence of her mother's restorative skills that I am filled with wonder. A *loved* book, this.

The Owl and the Pussy-cat   Edward Lear, illus. Gwen Fulton
(Faber/Piccolo paperback)

'The sooner the better' is the rule for introducing children to
Lear's incomparable nonsense rhymes, and Gwen Fulton's illustrations have precision and clarity, as well as originality, and
sure use of colour. The paperback edition is a good size for
handbag or car – I would keep an extra copy. You will know
the famous rhyme by heart in no time, and can use it, along
with familiar nursery rhymes, in a host of different situations.

Welcome, Little Baby   Aliki   (Bodley Head)

One cannot imagine a better present for new parents than this
enchanting and yet realistic little book. Ten double spreads and
one last single page combine to welcome a new baby, tell her
what to expect from the world in the way of basic satisfactions
('You'll learn to walk, to run, to talk, to read . . .') and guarantee, implicitly, the love and support of family and friends.
Sharing such a book with a small child who has just turned into
a big brother or sister could help understanding and acceptance,
as well as give pleasure. The delicate, gently detailed pictures
are totally complementary to the minimal text; and the endpapers are perfect.

When I was One . . .

3

When I was One,
I had just begun.

In the second year of life, children are transformed from babies into people. With minimal help or direction, normal children arrive at their second birthday able to move around their world, manipulate objects, and make their needs and feelings known. Any group of two year olds demonstrates the capacity of the human being to develop, apparently spontaneously.

But the similarity of two-year-old children is more apparent than real; a startling diversity is revealed on closer contact. There was a stage, about forty years ago, when experts would have told us with confidence that IQ, a supposedly inborn and unchangeable quality, was responsible for these differences. Nowadays, opinion is more guarded. Children are certainly born with a 'potential', although this is impossible to assess and, the psychologists assure us, never fully realized even in a superbly successful life.

The real differences relate to the individual conditions of the children themselves, and in each case this condition is the product of inherited factors *and* upbringing – 'nature and nurture' as the combination is often called. For all working purposes, we can assume that 'nature' has equipped the normal child with all he or she needs. It is 'nurture' that concerns us, because this is what *we* provide.

What next, then, for the year-old baby who is already used to nursery rhymes, jingles, 'naming' books and anything else that we have wanted to try?

Increasingly, she will want and need to handle her own books, as well as to look and listen while others perform. In fact, the more opportunity babies have to develop and refine their handling skills, the more cheerfully will they accept the role of passive listeners and observers during read-aloud sessions.

It is a sensible scheme, once the baby is toddling, to keep a number of books on horizontal surfaces – low tables and ledges – as well as to preserve some larger, more expensive books by consigning them to the safety of shelves. It should be expected and accepted that the accessible books will be used by the baby. This means that she will sort through them, carry them around, pull some on to the floor to 'read' and generally make this book-contact part of her life. This is important; ideally, the adults in the house will have their 'everyday' books within arm's reach, too. At a very early age 'passing Daddy's book' can be an exercise which gives both adult and child a glow of shared satisfaction, reinforces the notion that everyone reads and gives the baby practice in visual discrimination.

It is natural for some parents to be apprehensive about allowing the toddler such free access to books. If books have featured in their own lives as objects to be handled with great care, as expensive, luxury items rather than as everyday necessities, they may find it almost impossible to leave them lying around where the baby can get them.

If you feel like this, try making a connection in your mind between books and food. All parents know that children need nourishing food if their bodies are to grow lithe and healthy. They also know that older babies and toddlers must start to learn to feed themselves and that this will certainly lead to messiness, waste of food, and even damage to property. None the less, they allow the child to learn; to embark on the bumbling practice which will lead to that dexterity with knife, fork and spoon which our society expects and demands.

Books are as essential for the developing mind as cereal, fruit and vegetables are for the growing body. In an environment where books are valued and used, competence is achieved early.

When Anthony was exactly thirteen months old, his mother wrote in her diary: 'Today, for the first time, I saw Anthony go through a book turning over one page at a time. Formerly, he has turned several together, with the occasional separate one. He seemed to know exactly what he was doing . . .' The day before, he had, for the first time, spontaneously 'spoken' a word from the text. Opening *The Animals of Farmer Jones* at random, he had come upon the picture of the cow, underneath which is written:

> *'Moo, moo,' says the cow.*
> *'I am very hungry.'*

'Moo-oo,' said Anthony, gazing earnestly at the page. Later, his mother asked him to 'go and get your book about Farmer Jones'. He found it, even though the floor was littered with books, and brought it across the room for her to read to him.

Of course there will be some damage, even the odd catastrophe. We still talk about the time one of our own staggering babies hurled not one but *two* valued picture books into the bath where his older sister was being scrubbed. He had the best of intentions, we assured our tearful daughter. He knew she loved those books! Expectation of wear and tear is part of the contract we all make when we embark on parenthood. Why should books – essential family equipment – be seen as 'different' in some way? Or, even worse, as unnecessary equipment!

Recollection of my own family's involvement with books convinces me that books are surprisingly durable, given minimal adult supervision. Somehow, years after the dolls and cars and tricycles have all disappeared, there are Mike Mulligan, Little Tim and Babar standing shoulder to shoulder on the shelf, welcoming the renewed life which visiting grandchildren offer.

'Little books for little hands' is a maxim worth testing at this point. It is almost impossible for a baby to turn a large page without some damage, whereas a small, squarish leaf seems to flip over safely. The Pieńkowski and Bruna titles mentioned earlier are heaven-sent for beginning book-handlers and there are several other series worth investigating. The best of these are listed at the end of this, or the next chapter. Series should never be used indiscriminately, however. Often, the standard varies surprisingly from book to book, and levels are similarly unreliable. The titles may appear to be of equal difficulty, and yet be widely different in the demands they make on a child's understanding and maturity.

When considering material for this early age group, it is as well to recognize the distinction between 'theme' and 'story' books. Stories, for any age group, have narrative; the characters are established, and then the action starts. There is a plot, with some sort of climax and resolution, and it is necessary for the reader to carry the action step by step in the mind as the tale unfolds. This requires considerable mental expertise, and this expertise cannot be assumed to be present automatically. Why should we imagine that the baby of fifteen months will naturally know that the teddybear on the second page of the book is the same as appeared on the first? I learned this early: 'More teddybear!' (meaning another teddybear, or rabbit, or puppy or whatever) said my first child every time I turned the page. This was the same child who, at three (see Chapter 4), was dismayed and upset by the apparent disappearance of Patapon the sheep's 'seven little lambs'. For some children, what is pictured is real, always.

'Theme' books are less demanding, but are still a step ahead of 'naming' books, which depict unconnected objects. A 'theme' book depicts objects, activities and situations which are connected in some way. Pieńkowski's *Sizes* with, on successive pages, 'big lady little boy', 'big whale little fish', 'big mountain little hill', is a good example, as are other titles in this series, mentioned in Chapter 2. In each, a theme is explored, but the reader does not need to know what went before to make sense of any one opening.

Thomas is Little by Gunilla Wolde betrays its modern origin in its conscious teaching of adjectives, but is a simple and attractive little book of the same kind. It describes a small boy's equipment and activities. Thomas's teddy is 'warm, squashy and *soft*', whereas his wooden lorry is '*hard* and red and shiny'. Other Thomas books are similarly useful, though several are more advanced in concept. They are listed in appropriate sections.

The series 'Small World' by Leila Berg and Lisa Kopper includes titles such as *Cars*, *Ducks* and – with originality – *Vacuum Cleaners* and *Blood and Plasters*. These are colourful, to-the-point little 'theme' books with brief, but never mundane texts. 'Ducks are always glad to see you. That is the very best thing about them.'

A rather special 'theme' book deserves mention at this stage. If your baby is adopted, you would do well to pave the way for later explanation and discussion with a splendid little book aimed squarely at the smallest listener. *I Am Adopted* by Susan Lapsley is a tiny book, with realistic, simple but appealing illustrations by Michael Charlton. Its intention is merely to familiarize the child with the word 'adopted'. Nothing is more certain than that adopted children hear this term long before anyone thinks they are old enough to understand. Not understand, perhaps, but old enough to feel apprehensive about labelling ... This little volume puts adoption clearly on the credit side of the balance sheet.

> My name is Charles.
> I am adopted,

says a confident little boy, looking at a book in bed, with his teddy at his side. Later, riding his tricycle with verve,

> Do you know what adopted means?
> I do.

Charles and his small sister Sophie live a warm and happy family life, with parents, friends, a dog, a doting Granny, a rabbit ...

> It means we were given to Mummy and Daddy
> when we were little.
> And they brought us home to make a family.

Adoption here is equated with belonging; with being loved, and having fun. Association of ideas is important. Be sure, if your child is adopted, that he or she *feels* good about it from earliest days. The sensation will cling, when they begin to understand. (For your own delectation, examine both front and back endpapers of *I Am Adopted*. They tell a mute but eloquent story.)

Another theme which is likely to demand coverage at this (or any other) time in your child's life, is the imminence of a new brother or sister. It is desirable to try to prepare the child for this intrusion, however young he may be, and a book *always* helps.

The New Baby by Althea will be enjoyed in its own right, and, with repeated readings, may even entrench the notion that the family really is about to be increased, that the newcomer is inside Mum at the moment, and that good as well as bad features may be expected to characterize his or her arrival. There is a picture of a doctor examining a recumbent expectant mum's bulge, and another of her breastfeeding the baby. Nothing more explicit is shown or described; the rest of the book deals with the care of the baby, and its assimilation into the family's pattern of life.

There is a useful category of books which sits on the fence between the pure theme book and the true story. It has a confident foot in each field, and is indispensable as a launching pad for story proper. One might perhaps call these 'descriptive' books.

Sarah Garland has made an outstanding contribution to this category with four short, splendidly earthy books: *Doing the Washing*, *Going Shopping*, *Having a Picnic* and *Coming to Tea*. Each volume depicts a calm-in-the-circumstances Mum of gratifying ordinariness, a small girl, younger toddler and large dog, all engaged in the everyday pursuits of the titles. The toddler works with dedicated originality to sabotage constructive accomplishment on all fronts, and the dog clearly does not know its place. The little girl is superb, a match for any situation; and the toddler will come up trumps too, one feels. How could he fail, with a mother whose strength and humour shine through all? As good for parents as children, these brisk and eloquent books. Sarah Garland's art style had a kind of fly-away vigour which is none the less generous in detail and always comprehensible, and her use of colour is sure and generous.

Translating everyday life into print and picture for the very, very young seems, at the moment, to be largely the preserve of a small but growing group of women author-artists, of whom Sarah Garland is one. Jan Ormerod is another and her books are described in end-of-chapter lists. One suspects that most men still lag in that total awareness of small children which women in our society have traditionally shown; an awareness which reveals itself as much in depiction of physical attitude – the set of a leg, the tilt of a head, the way a child's body works when it sits, crouches, or runs – as in careful attention to features. One can believe that, as more men take over the everyday (and every night!) care of their young children, the field will be more equally served by the sexes.

One never knows; perhaps the trend may even be reversed. (After all no one draws children from whom more feeling emanates than Quentin Blake – and Edward Ardizzone, born in 1900, has left behind him an army of real, live, *feeling* children, from babies up.)

Undisputed modern master in the field is Shirley Hughes; and she is seen at her best in her 'Nursery Collection', published by Walker Books. I would buy all six of these incomparable, fortunately inexpensive little volumes. Entitled severally *Bathwater's Hot*, *When We Went to the Park*, *Noisy*, *All Shapes and Sizes*, *Colours*, and *Two Shoes*, *New Shoes*, each is a celebration of child and babyhood. The paraphernalia of family life, indoors and out, invades each page; the children are enterprising, honest, ordinary and full of that heartbreaking charm which is the true quality of childhood, and which has nothing to do with prettiness and good behaviour. As always, design and use of colour are masterly.

A Japanese author and artist team, Shigeo Watanabe and Yasuo Ohtomo, have produced, over recent years, a series of very simple picture books which are just right for children between one and two. With titles like *I'm going for a walk!*, *I can build a house!* and *How do I put it on?* these are uniformly satisfying books. Between the covers, a very young bear faces the physical and social problems common to the second year of life – as well as revelling in its satisfactions. The clarity of Ohtomo's illustrative style is hard to describe: his colours are quiet and few, his background the consistent white of the page. A gentle warmth is conveyed – and the subject matter is totally appropriate.

I wonder who first thought of using a small flap attached to a page to conceal and then reveal a person, animal or object, to the delight of the viewer? We will probably never know, though I suspect that early examples have passed without the acclaim accorded several modern ones. The device is simple, and the resulting book more durable than the complicated 'pop-up', with its tabs to pull and wheels to turn.

With the creation by Eric Hill of an appealing puppy called Spot, the technique sprang to public attention, so that 'Spot' books are now found, appropriately translated, in the far corners of the world. Spot books are instantly recognizable; square in shape, with sensibly stiff pages, they present animals and objects in pleasing and simple clarity against a white background. Best of all, there is the expected flap at every opening, to be lifted triumphantly, revealing such delights as a monkey eating a banana (in a wardrobe, where we are expecting to find Spot himself) or a tortoise, under a rug (where we were *certain*, from the shape of the bump, that we would find the errant puppy at last).

Subsequent titles show the guileless puppy in a variety of situations, from school to the circus. All are successful and the large, clear, simple text is excellent for early reading at a later stage. To my mind, the original *Where's Spot?* has never quite been equalled, but each new book has adult enthusiasts rushing to acquire it for the young devotees in their care.

The recipe has, predictably, been copied, and several of these other 'flap' books have achieved (lesser) prominence. My granddaughter Charlotte, at just two, finds *Oh Dear!* by Rod Campbell so uproariously funny that I am amazed, all over again, at the way in which children do not change. A small boy, sent to fetch an egg from the farmyard, finds instead a succession of other objects behind and through the doors and windows he hopefully opens. Charlotte's shriek of delighted hilarity at the raising of each flap would warm the heart of the author, could he but hear it. One can, of course, see the child's point: given that she knows that eggs come from chickens, the suggestion that a cow or a pig might produce one is likely to raise a laugh. But ten times over? 'Oh yes,' the parents of second-year babies will tell you resignedly. 'If it works once, it will work *fifty* times.'

You will, of course, come to feel that these simple little books are all very well for the baby, but ultimately a little boring for you. Such parental rebellion is to be encouraged. This is the right time to join the local library, if you don't belong already.

Membership of a library allows you to experiment, and experimentation often leads to the emergence of unexpected truths. Be reckless; bring home anything that you fancy, or want to investigate. You'll have to bow to your child's choice in a year or two, so you may as well have fun while the field is yours. You may find that your toddler's gaze is held compulsively captive by bold, dramatic slabs of colour in a book which is still several years beyond her understanding. On no account be persuaded that the text, because it is 'too hard', should not be read aloud. Modern research shows that children who are exposed to complex speech patterns learn to express themselves earlier and more fluently than those who are spoken to in careful, simple sentences. But the child's willingness to listen, meanwhile enjoying the pictures and the special feelings of warmth and sharing which read-aloud sessions evoke, must call the tune. If she doesn't enjoy the experience, your persistence will do more harm than good. But don't form hasty conclusions about what is suitable without trying a variety of types.

A real strength at this early stage is rhyme, and an impressive number of artists have conspired to exploit its undoubted appeal. One can believe that the opportunities presented by 'The House that Jack Built' or 'Mary Had a Little Lamb' might prove irresistible to an artist who longed to indulge his passion for colour and line, and at the same time communicate with the very young. For freshness and enthusiasm this audience is unmatched anywhere.

William Stobbs has elevated the old tale of Jack and his house – malt, maiden, priest and all – to the ranks of high artistic and literary achievement, and Tomie de Paola's evocation of Mary and her lamb has the perfection of a small cameo (Mary, sitting cross-legged in the attic reading, with faithful lamb recumbent at her side will be savoured at each session).

'Over in the Meadow' is probably the most lulling number rhyme ever composed – and one supposes that it must have been composed originally, though its modern forms are diverse. The factor they all have in common is a wonderfully warm, drowsy contentment.

> *Over in the Meadow in the sand in the sun*
> *Lived an old mother turtle and her little turtle one.*
> *'Dig' said the Mother,*
> *'I dig' said the one;*
> *So he dug and was glad in the sand in the sun.*

'Over in the Meadow' is not to be missed. An old version by John Langstaff, with illustrations by Feodor Rojankovsky, was a favourite in my own family for many years; it must have endured hundreds of read-aloud sessions and is, indeed, still in our library. And Ezra Jack Keats' version is superb, too. The warm colours of a summer afternoon drench 'the little crows six' and 'the little crickets seven' in a haze of peace and plenty, and communicate their glow to reader and listener alike. Sadly, both of these versions are out of print at the moment, but the library may be able to help.

Just arrived on the scene is a version which, in its own different way, will delight. By Olive A. Wadsworth, with pictures by Mary Maki Rae, this version is bolder in presentation than the older books, with brilliant slabs of colour as background to engaging, easily discerned and counted animals. But I miss the eloquence of the wording in the old, Langstaff edition. Why 'dug all day' when 'dug and were glad' invites the young listener to share in the joy of living experienced by the 'little turtle one', 'the little ducks nine'? Perhaps this is to split hairs; the endpapers of this book are a joy to peruse, with centrally placed picture of the meadow ringed with, in turn, the boxed numerals from 1 to 10, each followed by its appropriate animal. This allows the child to recap the listening experience with '1 turtle, 2 fish, 3 owls, 4 rats . . .' and, in all likelihood, to begin to recognize numbers in their written form.

At this early stage, rhyme helps in yet another more practical way. Once the baby has mastered the art of page-turning, he will be intent upon demonstrating his accomplishment. You'll be lucky if you *can* read the text before the page is turned! Knowing it by heart is almost essential, and rhymes are easiest to learn. Of course, traditional rhymes are usually known at least in part beforehand.

This is the stage when one-page-per-rhyme Mother Goose books have a clear advantage over the 'bigger' type. Bantam publishes three excellent, purse-sized little volumes, and Little Golden Books usually have a 'Mother Goose' in print.

This second year is the time, too, for wordier A B Cs and counting books, and there is an agreeable and increasing number of these available.

The Very Hungry Caterpillar cannot fail to delight and amaze. It has everything. At the first two openings, we meet a little egg, which quickly hatches a 'tiny and very hungry caterpillar'. The rest of the book tells the tale of the caterpillar's increasing and cheerful gluttony, as he eats his way through three plums, four strawberries, five oranges . . . to final repletion. At last, stomachache and all, he builds a cocoon around himself, retires, and after 'more than two weeks', emerges as a 'beautiful butterfly'.

This extraordinary book (which has been imitated but never, of its type, approached in excellence) is simultaneously a counting book, a nature lesson, a painless Monday-to-Sunday exposition, and to cap it all, a 'manipulative' book; the finger-sized hole in each edible object on successive sturdy pages invites immediate exploration. But the whole is more than the sum of the parts. Its impact is sobering in its force. An argument for acquiring the hard-cover edition lies in the certainty of its endurance among front-line family favourites for years. *The Very Hungry Caterpillar* demands to be learned by heart. Performances will still be given at five and six, when 'by heart' material plays a valuable role in learning to read.

Less spectacular, but just as innovative, is Susanna Gretz's *Teddybears 1 to 10*. Why are teddybears so enduringly appealing? Successive double spreads devoted to '1 teddybear, 2 old teddybears, 3 dirty old teddybears . . .' with the described characters depicted in colour against white backgrounds, sprawling dazedly or whirling dizzily (in a washing machine – nothing Edwardian about *these* bears) enchant utterly. At eighteen months, Sam, my eldest grandson, used to gaze as if mesmerized until the last page, on which '. . . 10 teddybears home for tea' pose for their photograph in a large armchair . . . except for one, who has fallen down the back and is seen as two desperate eyes and a pair of clutching paws. 'Peep-bo!' Sam would shout in glee, bringing his face to within an inch of the discomfited bear!

The bears reappear in *Teddybears ABC*, in which they are seen 'arriving in an aeroplane', 'climbing', 'dancing', 'finding fleas in their fur' and 'mucking about in the mud'. Wonderful, alliterative phrases to be absorbed now, and laughed at later.

Dr Seuss's ABC might well be acquired in the second year of life (preferably in hard covers; it lies flatter, that way). The jingly nonsense will appeal to the baby's sense of fun and encourage you

to bounce, tickle and generally indulge her; and it is never too
soon to start using the sounds of the alphabet in a way which is
likely to stick:

> *Big R*
> *little r*
> *Rosy Robin Ross.*
> *Rosy's going riding*
> *on her*
> *red rhinoceros.*

Dr Seuss's clownish little characters have a determined affability
about them which is hard to resist. This will become a much used
and quoted book.

Years ago I used to read my children the Lear Alphabet which
begins 'A was once an apple pie' from the old *Faber Book of Nursery
Verse* (happily, reissued). In time, I had it by heart, and would
often say it without the book, with family chorus supporting lustily.
Now available in picture-book form, this wonderfully nonsensical,
rhyming alphabet will evoke a sure response from second-year
babies – and their elders. There is no 'suitable' age for such a
book; its appeal is to the senses, not the intellect.

> *A was once an apple pie,*
> *Pidy*
> *Widy*
> *Tidy*
> *Pidy*
> *Nice insidy*
> *Apple Pie!*

The illustrations by Carol Newsom seem to rollick through the
pages of this picture-book version with expansive good humour.
Such an earnest undertaking as 'learning the alphabet' need never
feature consciously, for the child exposed to Lear's robust fun.
Perusal of successive spreads reveals an exuberant little mouse of
portly proportions, always involved in the (improbable) action.
The text is particularly clear and well-set, preceded by both capital
and small letter as appropriate, the page further embellished with
upper and lower case ornamental letter. The characters have spirit

and originality and include 'Great King Xerxes' who made his mark in our family. When he was about eleven, one of our sons came home after a history lesson at school one day and said to me, 'We've just met up with Great King Xerxes. I always thought you made him up!'

This sort of book illustrates the superior effect of rich, flowing sound over mundane *sense* for babies and toddlers. There is a tendency among publishers to produce, in response to a growing demand for titles for the very young, books which are over-earnest to the point of dullness. We need to remember that the sound rather than the sense of language is all important if babies are to be 'hooked'. Later, at nearly two, they will be enthralled by the evidence that life goes on between the covers of a book. Meanwhile rhythm, rhyme and the peculiar satisfactions which arise from sound used resonantly will evoke a ready response, arousing an expectation of satisfaction, even joy. Compare Lear's Alphabet ('Waddly-woosy Little Goose!') with 'Sally likes to skip. The boys fly their kites.' Neither text can mean much to the year-old baby – but Lear's will set her feet jigging and her senses soaring – and bring her back for more.

But Where is the Green Parrot? is a phenomenon; it does not belong in any category. Each page shows a different background (a train, a toy chest, a table set for tea), lists the objects pictured therein, and asks in capital letters: 'BUT WHERE IS THE GREEN PARROT?' There he is, in each case peeping from behind, below, above or through, a unifying and satisfying character who elevates this book to a level far above the earnest little volumes which in their dismal dozens invite children to 'point' and 'name' as a way of learning. Thomas and Wanda Zacharias do not hesitate to present their tree 'heavy with red apples . . .', to equip their horse with 'tight curls, a blue bridle with yellow tassels, a rider in the saddle with high boots . . .' But then, they probably had no intention of 'teaching' children anything.

There is another comparison to be made between those books which are intentionally instructive, and those which imaginatively represent the world. The former state, page after page, bold, boring and obvious truths about shops, sunshine, school or any other natural or man-made phenomenon. The latter estabish atmosphere through interrelating picture and language, evoking response on several fronts: emotional and artistic as well as intellectual.

A small, rather overlooked volume by Cynthia Mitchell, illustrated by Satomi Ichikawa, springs to mind. Its author has, with deceptive ease, assembled fifty-six participles to describe children's playtime activities. The words sprawl across the page with a vigour which matches the energy of the robust and cheerful children described. They are revealed '. . . hopping, jumping, bouncing, bumping . . .' as well as '. . . fighting, falling, sprawling, bawling . . .' The expressive, rhythmical words are matched by explicit, softly coloured but spirited pictures. It is called, simply and appropriately, *Playtime*.

And this is the time for the old woman and her recalcitrant pig! A modern version by Priscilla Lamont, *The Troublesome Pig*, retains the original rhythm of this rousing old tale, and demonstrates the power of unrhymed verse to enthral:

> '*Please water, quench fire,*
> *Then fire will burn stick,*
> *Stick will beat dog,*
> *Dog will bite pig,*
> *The pig will jump over the stile*
> *And we shall get home tonight!*'
>
> *But would the water quench the fire?*

IT WOULD NOT.

The pictures in this book capture the spirit of the story and impart true individuality to all the characters. The text makes compulsive listening, and unfamiliar words – stile, harness, quench, gnaw – will be stored up for future reference, as more and more traditional rhymes and tales are encountered.

You may notice that the artist has used a delicate rather than vigorous style to embellish the old tale; the colours are muted and sensitive rather than bright and brash. You may wonder if very young children will attend to such pictures; have we not established that they prefer brilliant colours and lively pictures? I believe that this is like saying that, as young children obviously prefer ice cream to vegetables, we may as well defer to this taste and abandon our intention of providing them with good, nourishing food. In my experience, children increasingly enjoy a wide range of art styles if we give them the chance, and the example of our own appreciation.

In the few years that have elapsed since its appearance, *The Baby's Catalogue* by Janet and Allan Ahlberg has become an established feature of the 'Books for Babies' scene. The first page of this truly enchanting book introduces the six babies whose lives become its subject, in catalogue form. They represent five families; two of the babies are twins. Each successive page is appropriately labelled: Toys, Brothers and Sisters, Dinners, Games . . . In each case one can differentiate the babies and their families, with details compounding as the book proceeds. Endless perusal is rewarded by discovery, the 'Books' page strikes a blow for the right cause and 'Accidents' ought to become a poster for framing. These babies are babies, in all their messy and appealing innocence. They are celebrated gloriously here, in a book which seems certain to survive into the next century.

As I complete the revision of this chapter, a book has just fallen into my lap which I immediately recognize as a potential winner in the toddler stakes. It is *Cock-a-Doodle-Doo*, with words by Franz Brandenberg and pictures by Aliki, his wife. One might call it a farm book, a noise book, a family book . . . light, warmth and happiness arise from its pages, with animals and humans pursuing their active course through an early morning stint of milking, chicken-feeding and breakfast preparation. There is much more in the expansive, truly enchanting pictures than the simple text reveals, but no over-cleverness, no contrivance. The small child's eye will find plenty to look at, nothing to confuse in these pages. (I have just read it aloud to Bridget, fourteen months old. Her usual determination to help turn pages was in total abeyance for once, her eyes straying with attention across the wide, landscape double spreads. My loud 'oinks' and 'neighs' were received soberly and, I think, appreciatively.)

Such a book is an experience, from which a child will derive immediate and lasting benefit. Experiences lodge in the mind and heart, and enrich the spirit – unlike lessons, which as often as not, bounce off and are lost. Spend your baby's second year of life entrenching and expanding the book habit you have established in the first year. If you have been really successful, of course, it won't feel as if you are implementing any policy; you and your child will both know, with assurance, that books are indispensable and that the good life you are leading together is immeasurably enriched by their cheerful and comforting presence.

Book List 2
Books to use between One and Two

Remember to use this list in conjunction with Book List 1 (page 27) and to consult Book List 3 (page 81) for very bookwise children.

All Gone!
All Clean!
Run! Run!
Cock-a-Doodle-Doo! all by Harriet Ziefert, illus. Harriet Drescher (Heinemann)
> These four books fall peripherally into the 'noise' category in that each, in its different way, invites adult performance. The illustrations are vivid and exuberant, the text scant. The six words, 'Horses whinny, Geese honk, Sheep . . . baa!' take reader and listener to the end of the fourth double spread, with plenty of time for perusal and extra sound effects. And for learning? Between the four books I counted forty-one animals after subtracting repetitions!

Baby Bear's Bedtime (and *Good Morning, Baby Bear*) Eric Hill (Heinemann)
> Both these small, square volumes are true first story books. An exuberant, simply drawn little bear makes his cheerful way through the day, and off to bed, to the accompaniment of a good book read aloud by Mummy Bear. Flat, bright colours against white backgrounds, with brief text following the action, render both books perfect for second-year babies.

* *The Baby's Catalogue* Janet and Allen Ahlberg (Viking Kestrel/Puffin paperback)
* *Bathwater's Hot* (and *When We Went to the Park*, *Noisy*, *All Shapes*

and Sizes, Colours and *Two Shoes, New Shoes*)   Shirley Hughes
(Walker)

A Bookload of Animals   Maureen Roffey   (Bodley Head)
In twelve satisfying double spreads, this book uses sixty-three
words to state twelve trite-but-true similes: 'as Big as an Elephant' . . . 'as Slow as a Snail' . . . 'as Crafty as a Cartload of
Monkeys' and 'as Mad as a March Hare'. The collage illustrations are memorable; I should like the Dog, in his utter Faith-
fulness, framed on my wall. Unfortunately this is out of print
but you should find a copy in your library.

The Big Blue Truck (and *The Busy Orange Tractor, The Little Red
Car, The Noisy Green Engine, The Strong Yellow Tug Boat*)   Rosalinda
Kightley   (Walker)
Appropriately called 'On the Move' board books, these are
robust little volumes with a strong noise component: 'Hiss! went
the air. Slurp! went the oil.' One line of text only, at the foot of
each page, bold colour, brisk and assertive little characters:
formula for success.

Brinkworth Bear's Counting Book   Annie West   (Macdonald)
A sound, square little volume which appeals at first encounter.
Numerals (1 to 12) are large and clear and pictures attractive.
An added factor is the smooth alliteration of the captions: 'five
fancy fish', 'ten tiny teapots', 'and eleven elegant elephants'.
Back to the beginning for a second – or third – reading!

Buster's Morning and *Buster's Afternoon*   Rod Campbell   (Blackie)
Two small books about the same small boy who searched for an
egg in *Oh Dear!* (page 44). The same 'flap' device has him
peering over fences, into cupboards and through windows, scrab-
bling under the cabbages and finally cuddling down for a rest
under a 'flap' quilt. Clarity and brevity are the keynote in these
splendid little books.

*But Where is the Green Parrot?   Thomas and Wanda Zacharias
(Chatto & Windus/Piccolo paperback)

*Cars (and *Ducks, Vacuum Cleaners* and *Blood and Plasters*)   Leila
Berg and Lisa Kopper   (Methuen)

The Chicken Book   Anon, illus. Garth Williams   (Patrick Hardy/
Picture Lions paperback)

Said the first little chicken,
With a queer little squirm,
I wish I could find
A fat little worm!

Best known to American children perhaps, though my children had it from babyhood, source unknown. Garth Williams's disconsolate chickens (five) are cuddlesome, his backgrounds uncluttered.

Now see here, said the mother,
From the green garden patch,
If you want any breakfast,
Just come here and SCRATCH!

Lesson learned, laughter assured.

*Cock-a-Doodle-Doo Franz Brandenberg, illus. Aliki (Bodley Head/Piccolo paperback)

Dad's Back (also *Messy Baby*, *Reading* and *Sleeping*) Jan Ormerod (Walker)

The special feature of this 'Baby Book' series is its concentration on fathers: not a Mum in sight! Text is confined to one or two words on a page. Illustration is all, and is more than enough. Jan Ormerod's babies sit, crawl, wriggle and haul themselves about in a way which has authenticity, complete and utter. Adults will laugh aloud; but the pictures are clear enough for children, too.

*Dr Seuss's ABC Dr Seuss (Collins/Collins paperback)

*Doing the Washing (and *Going Shopping*, *Having a Picnic* and *Coming to Tea*) Sarah Garland (Bodley Head/Puffin paperback)

Each Peach Pear Plum Janet and Allen Ahlberg (Viking Kestrel/Picture Lions paperback)

An 'I Spy' book in which the child is invited to find familiar nursery rhyme characters hiding in the deftly drawn and neatly framed illustrations.

Tom Thumb in the cupboard
I spy Mother Hubbard

Mother Hubbard down the cellar
I spy Cinderella

The interiors are meticulously drawn, the exterior scenes filled with the light of summer afternoons. Each left-hand page has not only text (framed, like the illustrations), but an engaging little picture-heading.

*An Edward Lear Alphabet   Edward Lear, illus. Carol Newsom (Angus and Robertson)

*The Faber Book of Nursery Verse   Barbara Ireson (ed.)   (Faber paperback)

Farm Counting Book   Jane Miller   (Dent)
This is a photographic picture book in which considerable care has been taken to keep backgrounds clear and uncluttered. The objects themselves from 'one kitten' to 'ten geese' with splendid red numerals provided as well, are distinct and attractive. Bright yellow borders lend colour and clarity. (See Book List 4 for companion volume, Farm Alphabet Book, which is more complex in concept.)

Farming with Numbers   Maureen Roffey   (Bodley Head)
A farming family and a description of its daily life is cumulatively built up, from 'one farmhouse' through 'five cows' (Lulu, Jenny, Daisy, Rosie and Bell) to 'ten fields, side by side'. The satisfying sturdy characters and animals, stylized and recognizable against their uncluttered backgrounds, can be identified, counted and re-checked by an older pre-schooler. The toddler will enjoy the repetition and savour the bright, flat colours long before understanding of some of the terms is possible. Unfortunately this is out of print at present but you should be able to obtain a copy from your library.

*The House that Jack Built   illus. William Stobbs   (Oxford)

How Many?   Fiona Pragoff   (Gollancz)
It is almost impossible not to exclaim aloud at the clarity and beauty of the photographs in this arresting, spiral-bound, wipe-clean little book. Successive double spreads range from one (solid, old-fashioned) key, to twenty (youthful, tanned) toes. Everyone will have their favourite. Mine are five pairs of vividly coloured, variously patterned socks for '10' and fifteen round, square or triangular buttons, in a perfect, flat pyramid. '17 teddybears' belie description (and would certainly be hard to

count – but who cares? Babies can't count anyway.). My copy is
going with Bridget (seventeen months) on her first plane trip. A
perfect companion.

I Am Adopted Susan Lapsley, illus. Michael Charlton (Bodley
Head)

I'm going for a walk! (and *Hallo! How are you?*, *How do I eat it?*, *How
do I put it on?*, *I can build a house!*, *I can do it!*, *I'm having a bath with
Papa!*, *I'm the king of the Castle!*, *I'm playing with Papa!* and *Ready,
Steady Go!* Shigeo Watanabe, illus. Yasuo Ohtomo (Bodley
Head/Puffin paperback)

Mary Had a Little Lamb illus. Tomie de Paola (Andersen
Press/Beaver Books paperback)

My Cat Likes to Hide in Boxes Eve Sutton, illus. Lynley Dodd
(Hamish Hamilton/Puffin paperback)

A succession of jaunty couplets about the cats of the world, with
some elegant and understated illustration, make this a successful
modern rhyming book.

My Day Rod Campbell (Collins/Picture Lions paperback)

This simple 'naming' book devotes ten double spreads to framed
pictures of objects which very young children will recognize.
Each page is divided neatly into quarters, so that eight objects
are revealed at each opening. Ten categories are covered, among
them 'inside the house', 'going shopping' and 'at the park'. At
each end of the book a toddler is shown getting up, and going to
bed. Treatment is representational rather than imaginative, and
colour is bright and clear. Single-word captions may be in-
dicated usefully by adult and, later, child. Such a book has a
place at rising-two, when most children like playing the recognition game.

The New Baby Althea (Souvenir Press)

Oh Dear! Rod Campbell (Blackie)

one panda: an Animal Counting Book Betty Youngs (Bodley
Head)

From 'one panda' to 'twelve seals', these fascinating pictures
will hold the eye of child and adult alike. This artist uses an
embroidery and appliqué technique to produce pictures of true
virtuosity. The animals are easily counted against their

backgrounds of colourful, coarse cloth, the appliquéd numerals and printed text clear and well placed. A long-life book,
this.

1, 2, 3, to the Zoo   Eric Carle   (Hamish Hamilton)
A large, brilliantly coloured counting book with an added feature: a small engine chugs along the bottom of each picture,
pulling, successively, carriages containing the animals already
pictured, in the numbers specified. At the very end, a wide fold-
out page reveals *all* the animals and birds installed in the zoo.
Limitless counting practice for the next few years – and fun to
look at and learn from now, with an obliging adult doing the
counting.

*Over in the Meadow   Ezra Jack Keats   (Scholastic)   Out of
print.

*Over in the Meadow   Olive A. Wadsworth, illus. Mary Maki
Rae   (Viking Kestrel)

A Peaceable Kingdom: The Shaker Abecedarius   illus. Alice and Martin
Provensen   (Viking Kestrel/Puffin paperback)

'ALLIGATOR, Beetle, Porcupine, Whale,
BOBOLINK, Panther, Dragonfly, Snail . . .' begins this old
(1882) and very individual animal alphabet. By the time the
whole irresistible cavalcade has been inspected, more than one
hundred animals, birds and fish (everyday, exotic and imaginary) have proceeded sedately across its wide, shallow pages.
Dignified ladies, gentlemen and children, all clad in Shaker
dress, reflect the sobriety and industry of this stern – but clearly
not dull – sect. The illustrations, against a buff-coloured background which evokes parchment, are sheer delight. Warmth
and good humour temper severity, and the details demand endless perusal.

A second-year baby, lucky enough to be introduced to this
'abecedarius' on parental knee, might well keep it in his head
and heart for life.

Pink Pigs in Mud: a Colour Book   Betty Youngs   (Bodley Head)
The author-artist here uses the same technique as distinguishes
her counting book, *one panda* (see above). This is a true 'theme'
book. It begins: 'Ted Hollins has a farm and on it there are . . .',

and then presents twelve double spreads of extraordinary and compelling beauty. One senses the loving work which has gone into this book; the front and back covers, enchanting endpapers and bonus title-page reveal Betty Youngs' determination to travel an extra mile towards excellence. This is not a 'showy' book and may be overlooked. Be sure to consider it!

Playtime Cynthia Mitchell, illus. Satomi Ichikawa (Heinemann)

Sam's Ball (and *Sam's Bath, Bad Sam!, Sam's Car, Sam's Biscuit, Sam's Teddy*) Barbro Lindgren, illus. Eva Eriksson (Methuen)

These must be the simplest stories ever written. Sam is clearly between one and two; his preoccupations, activities and reactions denote the second year of life, in all its single-track egotism. The simple statement on each left-hand page allows you to outdo your page-turning enthusiast, and make it to the end, triumphant. You will recognize your own irresponsible toddler in Sam, even though he or she doesn't. Sam himself is a homely change from the cherubs: you will like him.

See Mouse Run Sally Grindley, illus. Priscilla Lamont (Hamish Hamilton/Piccolo paperback)

A succession of farmyard animals run distractedly through the pages of this landscape-shaped book, each giving voice to its own oink, neigh or baa. The subject of their fright is revealed at the end as 'little Tommy Tasker going DRUM, DRUM, DRUM'. The pictures are gentle and expressive, and the text allows plenty of opportunity for adult and child to join in.

* *Teddybears 1 to 10*
* *Teddybears ABC* both by Susanna Gretz (Benn/Picture Lions paperback)

Ten Little Bad Boys Rodney Peppé (Viking Kestrel)

Ten spirited boys dispose of themselves in the best tradition in this vigorous version of the old rhyme. Peppé's exuberant and colourful pictures are suitably explicit (enchanting title-page illustration shows exactly the right number of pairs of trousers, socks and shirts for ten boys hanging on a line – with shoes beneath).

* *Thomas is Little* Gunilla Wolde (Hodder and Stoughton)

Touch and Feel abc Book   Margaret Chamberlain   (Methuen)

This tall, narrow board book has one agreeably clear and colourful picture for each lower-case letter: e for elephant, u for umbrella, and so on. The quality that makes it notable, however, is the way in which the letters are raised from the surface, by the use of brightly coloured felt. Baby fingers will want to feel the texture of the letters long before they sense their significance. Later, adult readers could demonstrate the ways in which the letters are conventionally printed, if they wished. The book is extremely well designed and sturdily made. It should give pleasure for years.

* *The Troublesome Pig* Priscilla Lamont   (Hamish Hamilton/ Piccolo paperback)

Trucks (also *Trains*, *Aeroplanes*, *Boats*)   Byron Barton   (Julia MacRae)

One cannot imagine a more suitable and joyful way of introducing the exciting world of moving vehicles to second-year babies. These splendid little books will, in all likelihood, be 'done to death' before their appeal ever fades. Fortunately, they are sturdy, with stiff, easy-to-turn pages. In each book, the recipe is repeated: a different example of the species is shown engaged in an occupation which is likely to interest young children, and reflect their world. One line of brief, clearly presented text runs across either bottom or top of the page:

> Here comes a tow truck towing a car.
> Here is a moving truck bringing the furniture.

The 'double-spread' approach allows a child to gaze at the page for as long as he or she wishes; and gazing is certainly justified. Clear, bright colour and crisp outline make a perfect job of the illustrations.

* *The Very Hungry Caterpillar* Eric Carle   (Hamish Hamilton/ Puffin paperback)

Where Have You Been? Margaret Wise Brown, illus. Barbara Cooney   (Scholastic)

Over thirty years old, and the work of two masters in the field, this is a true second-year book.

Little Old Cat
Little Old Cat
Where have you been?
To see this and that
Said the little Old Cat
That's where I've been.

Fourteen animals and birds are posed similar questions, and produce jaunty answers. The pages are beautifully designed, the pictures, in black, white and red, clear and expressive. Out of print now, it might be hard to find – but do try.

Where's the Bear? Charlotte Pomerantz, illus. Byron Barton (Julia MacRae)

A story told in forty words altogether – but in only seven, really! 'Where's the Bear?' occurs five times, 'There's the Bear' seven times, 'Where?' once alone, and 'There' twice alone. The seventh word is a triumphant/resigned/relieved 'Yeah!' at the end of this brilliantly understated, wonderfully depicted saga, as the protagonists peer from behind closed windows and the bear plods off in defeat. (He always looked more surprised than aggressive, anyway.) You will need several rehearsals to get your emphases right, but you and your youngster will love it on sight.

*Where's Spot? (and *Spot's First Walk, Spot's Birthday Party, Spot's First Christmas, Spot Goes to School, Spot Goes on Holiday,* and *Spot Goes to the Circus*)   Eric Hill   (Heinemann/Puffin paperback)

When I was Two . . .

4

When I was Two, I was nearly new

One can imagine a six-year-old, in retrospect, feeling with A. A. Milne that two was indeed a 'nearly new' time of life.

In fact, two-year-olds have learned more in volume since birth than they will ever learn again in a similar period. And they are ready for life. They want to open every door, take the tops off *all* the bottles and press *all* the switches. Successful parents of two-year-olds are identifiable by the ease with which they connive and conspire: to get their two-year-olds into bed, out of the bath, on to the pot, away from the fire, into a jersey, out of the china cabinet ... They develop a line of frenetically cheerful, non-stop patter which astounds and dismays their childless friends. It is of course aimed at diverting the young from occupations of their choice to occupations of their parents' choice. Just as naturally, the young resist diversion with vigour and outrage; there is nothing hypo-critical about the noises *they* make during the exchange.

The average two-year-old is athletic, voluble and determined. She assesses herself totally unrealistically, and can see no point of view but her own. Other people's rights do not exist, and she has no feeling for the relative importance of different people, places and things. Your best course is to hold on with as much good cheer as you can while she grows a little; and a little growth at this stage takes her a long way. She will, when you have all but given up, start to co-operate occasionally, modify her 'crashing through the jungle' life-style, show signs of understanding the rudiments of cause and effect, and even be prepared to wait a little while you make her a sandwich.

I have purposely avoided description of her attractive qualities.

Parents are inclined to smile through clenched teeth when their two-year-old's friendliness, and her deceptive appearance of shining and beautiful innocence, are remarked upon by visitors (who are not staying long, and are known to be returning to peaceful, tastefully arranged houses where books and music and good food mingle in pleasing and orderly proportion . . .).

Can you believe that *books* may make all the difference?

What the two-year-old lacks (particularly the first child in the family) is colour in her life. What *can* a two-year-old do to satisfy her burgeoning need for experience – for finding out how things look, how they feel, how they can be manipulated – *except* explore the possibilities of her surroundings? Her apparently diabolical intentions are, in fact, innocent, and her outrage at our interference (*she* thinks!) justified.

Constant recourse to books has, at this stage, as many advantages for the parent as for the child.

To begin with, book sessions fill in time, and time hangs heavy for both custodian and child in the early days. Granted, the adult has plenty to do, especially in a busy domestic situation, but the deterrent of a resident two-year-old may make productive accomplishment impossible a great deal of the time anyway, unless some way is found to meet her obtrusive needs. And you may as well, if you are going to be interacting with her most of the time, make the interaction as pleasurable as possible from your own point of view, as well as from hers.

And two-year-old books are fun!

In our family, a habit of taking to the sofa with books and babies after breakfast ('in the middle of the muddle') seems to have carried on into the second generation. By the time those who are departing to school or work have actually left, a break is needed; the toddler has had to defer to the pressing needs of older family members and is ready for attention. Half an hour of her own with her mother and a pile of books will set the tone for the rest of the morning, and make the mother's work not only easier to face, but less interrupted once begun. If there is a baby in the family, it may prove possible to feed her while this session proceeds, thereby ensuring that *her* earliest memories are of the associated warmths of milk and story. And be sure to include a special 'baby' book for her, consulting the older child about its choice and suit-ability. *Feeling* like an older brother or sister can have a lot to do with *behaving* like one.

Don't worry about leaving the dishes, or any other chore undone at this point; nothing is more certain than that the dishes *will* be washed and the next meal prepared, whereas no certainty at all attaches to the inclusion of story-sessions unless they are placed firmly at the top of the list. I've never been able to understand people who doggedly do the so-called 'essential' things first. If you have undertaken to assume a housekeeping role, you must, before all else, capitalize on the advantages; you are, after all, saddled with the drawbacks. And the one advantage that you have over most of the working world is that you can plan your work to suit yourself. Train yourself to smile confidently at neighbours' and relations' surprise or disapproval; tell them, if you need explain yourself at all, that you would be ashamed to neglect your children whereas you don't feel emotionally involved with the breakfast dishes. You will get through as much work as they, in the end, and the profits of your good sense will be as obvious to your critics as to yourself. With any luck, some of them, at least, will join you.

A word about the classic notion of 'the bedtime story'. This is usually envisaged idealistically, even sentimentally: dreamy child and adoring parent locked in a situation of wonder and rapport, with lights low and the rustlings of night all around.

You may achieve this (if you have household help, no other children, take the phone off the hook, and decide to relate *only* to this child, regardless of your own and other people's emotional and social needs). More probably, bedtime will be a fairly hectic period, with other family members making demands, nerves a little frayed all round, the child himself overtired and crotchety. If books have featured prominently during the day, you will have no need to feel any guilt about deciding to omit bedtime stories from your repertoire, at least temporarily. Once the child is old enough to accept that a story in bed is sometimes, but not always, possible, all will be well; but two-year-olds are not like this. Bedtime requires ritual – so be sure that you *can*, easily, perform the ritual every night before you institute it in an immutable form.

You might also, at this stage, consider looking about your neigh-
bourhood, town, or city, for a book group to join. The name and
nature of such groups vary (Books for Your Children Groups,
Children's Literature Associations, and so on) but most of them
are simply clubs whose members share an interest in books which
their children might enjoy. Don't feel that you need to know
about books already. All groups want, more than any other sort of
member, young (or older) parents who *don't know*, and want to *find
out* about books for their children. You will have something of
worth to contribute by reason of your current dealings with a
baby or small child. You are *really* 'in the field'! Even if you can't
attend meetings, joining is worthwhile. All such groups send out
material, accounts of meetings, lists of good books, and arrange
the occasional address by authors and artists. The more solitary
your life, the more you need to belong to organizations of people
who, like yourself, are tied up with child care, and concerned
about children's needs. Your local librarian should have information about such groups; or ask at the nearest school.

And so to books.

Between two and four the world opens up to the child. Whereas
before this time her curiosity was confined to her actual surroundings, she now wants, increasingly, to go out into the world,
to learn about everything, to become involved. She is able now to
follow a simple story through a book, and involve herself with the
characters. At two she will still love her 'old' books – repetition is
going to be savoured for a long time yet – but will need new and
different stories constantly.

Books like *Doing the Washing, How do I put it on?* and *Sam's Biscuit*
will have shown her that life goes on between the covers of a book.
Now she is ready to advance into other situations, to hear about
other people and things, likely and unlikely events.

With the growth of wider understanding, of course many of the
earlier books will assume new roles. Pleasure at the jingly rhythm
and bright pictures of *The House that Jack Built* and *Ten Little Bad
Boys* will be increased as more of the action is understood and the
people and objects 'tied up' with their counterparts in real life, or
in other books.

Fortunately, there has been an increase in the publication of simple but sound stories for two- to three-year-olds in the last few years; but you may still find difficulty in obtaining such books in any quantity. Appropriate books for this age group are often not seen by those who must market them as potentially successful; publishers, constantly on the lookout for a new *Where the Wild Things Are* or *Dogger*, may need to be persuaded that an apparently mundane little book about events in the restricted daily life of a two-year-old is not only well conceived and executed, but also likely to sell. The form of this type of book is, certainly, a demanding one, requiring as it does the provision of characters who come alive in situations which are believable, and action which *happens* – all within the experience or imagination of a human being whose knowledge of the world and its ways is only just beginning to widen.

Some of the best books are old or middle aged and may seem, to the adult who encounters them alongside the more glossy, colourful volumes of today, rather dull and dated. It is salutary to reflect that *Harry the Dirty Dog* by Gene Zion was published in 1956 and has been in print ever since. If one considers only colour and that indefinable 'modern' factor which seduces the eye before discernment intervenes, one is obliged to admit that Harry suffers by comparison. But look a little further: read *Harry the Dirty Dog* to a young child and you will recognize excellence.

Harry eclipses all dogs of fiction for the very young. The briskly related activities which transform him from a 'white dog with black spots' to a 'black dog with white spots' are rollicking in the extreme; this is how the small 'reader' would spend *his* day, given a temporary relaxation of adult supervision. Harry's 'family' is an anonymous group which exists only to support him, and provide a backdrop to his adventures.

Only Mr Gumpy has a name in the two books which celebrate his cheerful relationship with a large and irresponsible group of animals and humans (the pig, the rabbit, the boy, the girl). In the first title (*Mr Gumpy's Outing*) they all set out by water in Mr Gumpy's boat; in the second, *Mr Gumpy's Motor Car*, they are packed uncomfortably into a small ancient 'tourer'. In both books

they all (the guests, that is) behave badly, with predictably cata-
strophic consequences, but all is well in the end . . . Mr Gumpy's
affability is unfailing. Both stories end with a joyful gathering of all
the friends at Mr Gumpy's home.

Jeanne-Marie, her pets Patapon the sheep and Madelon the
duck and her friend Jean-Pierre have established their power to
captivate over a period of years. The text, translated from the
French, is more an excited commentary on the action than a
narrative. Its capacity to involve the small listener is considerable,
and the impact of the clear, colourful, doll-like characters, against
their white backgrounds, arresting and satisfying.

In this series, certain titles are more successful than others at
certain ages. *Jeanne-Marie Counts her Sheep* (fortunately borrowed
from the library) confused and upset my eldest child at first encounter when she was nearly three. She was clearly enchanted by
Jeanne-Marie's plans for the seven little lambs Patapon was expected to produce – they are shown on successive pages, in growing
numbers. But predictably, the little sheep gives birth to only one
lamb, and Catherine was not only mystified, but disturbed. 'What
has happened to the other little lambs?' was never answered to her
satisfaction at three, and we gave up. A year later, all was well.
Catherine's daughter Nicola gave evidence of exactly this confusion, years later. At a little over three she told friends happily,
'Our new baby is inside Mummy, and we don't know if it is a boy
or a girl. If it's a girl it will be Maria, and if it's a boy it will be
Samuel.' In due course, Samuel appeared and we all assumed
Nicola's total understanding. After all, she was both intelligent
and well informed. One day several months later she looked at her
mother with tragic eyes and asked 'Whatever happened to Maria?'
Obviously, Nicki could manage alternatives *verbally*, but not *actually*.

Early difficulties of this sort are not consistent from child to
child. Some (but certainly not all) children are confused by the
depiction of only part of a person or object, and most prefer everything mentioned to be pictured, a near impossible undertaking
once themes begin to expand. But it is surely reasonable to require
authors and artists to give care to such matters; and quite shocking

breaches are common. Sometimes the illustrations give the secret away and destroy the climax utterly. At other times pictures are blatantly incorrect, and show characters wearing the wrong clothes: shoes when the text has them barefooted, day clothes when pyjamas have been mentioned.

There is some evidence that with the growth of informed criticism, greater care is being given to these considerations. And yet the best of the old picture books – the ones which have endured – have always given meticulous care to the matching of text and illustration. (This factor is, of course, related to their endurance. I remember reading that Margaret Wise Brown, an inspired and abiding author, would change a word in her final text, if need be, to achieve union with her illustrator.)

Other problems are encountered as soon as we move into the realm of 'story'. How are we to know what will terrify and what amuse? We can't; each of us must find our own way through this maze, and none of us is likely to emerge without having turned into a wrong alley, and been obliged to back out hastily. Sometimes we can use our experiences to avoid later traps, but not always, and we run a risk in applying any rule too firmly. One of the greatest of these is that we will transfer our own trepidation to the child by our careful screening of situations and characters. Another is that we will become so assiduous in shielding the child from any situation which we suspect may frighten him, that his literary diet will become more and more insipid as the months roll by. And we cannot tell! I well remember one of my children always turning the page quickly to avoid listening to 'I had a Little Pony' (who was 'whipped' and 'slashed') and just as regularly shouting with delight when we reached 'Taffy was a Welshman' in which '. . . I took up the marrow bone and beat him on the head!' Clearly, for this child, violence against humans was less disturbing than violence against animals!

Another of our children, in the middle years of childhood, used to ask me to read *The Little Mermaid* aloud to her and then, halfway through, be so overcome that she would beg me to stop. By contrast, she showed nothing but gleeful enjoyment of ghosts, monsters, and the everyday violence which seems to invade the life of the modern child, regardless of parental vigilance. No conclusions have ever seemed possible in the light of such contradictory evidence.

Children between two and three are almost daily increasing their contact with the world and its fears, as well as its wonders. We cannot know how impression is building on impression to create the individual set of finely tuned reactions which will dicate their tolerance to events, people and circumstances. Certain simple precautions are sensible and easy to apply; beyond these, we must feel our way, using as guides our own sensitivity to the child's response and temperament.

Back to Françoise and Jeanne-Marie. Only *Springtime for Jeanne-Marie* is currently in print, though other titles may be available from libraries. *Springtime* is a prototype for all two- to three-year-old stories, I believe, and should not be missed. The story embodies the age-old lost-and-found theme. Jeanne-Marie and her pet sheep Patapon and her white duck Madelon go to pick flowers; Madelon, heedless of her mistress's warning, swims away down the river and is lost. Jeanne-Marie and Patapon pursue the little duck, meeting a succession of people who cannot help – and then a boy, Jean-Pierre, who can, and does. All is heart-warmingly resolved, the errant Madelon discovered unrepentantly alive, and a new friend made.

There is a substantial but jaunty air about the characters in all the Jeanne-Marie books. They give themselves over to unashamed emotion. Their behaviour is wholehearted. They are never devious or undecided. The page-sized pictures have a lucid, almost festive quality. They follow the action faithfully, and are beautifully complemented by the text, which is designed, rather than merely placed on the page. First published in the 1950s, *Springtime for Jeanne-Marie* demonstrates the power of certain books to captivate, certain characters to take on immortal life. This book, with its singular mixture of innocence and wisdom, joins *Harry the Dirty Dog*, *Mr Gumpy's Outing*, *The Tale of Peter Rabbit* and *The Elephant and the Bad Baby* at the top of the list. Each serves to demonstrate the rareness of the talent that can speak in real terms to this age group.

The under-threes like their characters to be consistent and de-pendable; and Jeanne-Marie, Harry and Mr Gumpy demonstrate these qualities to perfection. One knows, when the next title is opened, that Harry will embark upon another adventure in which his own energetic pigheadedness will lead him into trouble, Mr Gumpy will yet again allow his good nature to complicate his life and banish his comfort and Jeanne-Marie will once more plunge into some innocent and joyful celebration which, while its consequences may temporarily dismay her, will always renew her faith in life and its goodness in the end.

This is how stories for the under-threes should be; they should move smoothly in a steady direction to a predictable outcome. The best of them will contrive to achieve a sort of virtuosity which has the adult exclaiming, 'Yes. Just right,' to himself, the child listening and looking with that intent absorption which is reserved for the rare and superlative experience.

For this is what contact with a fine book can give to a very young child. Through it, he can experience the capacity of good English words to evoke emotion, to create place, and to usher the reader into that place. If this experience is offered him as a normal human right in childhood, he will expect repetition of it to the end of his life, and make sure that it is always available. In other words, he will become a reader.

Illustration interacts with text to produce this effect, of course, but it is the story and its telling on which the book stands or falls. Make no mistake about this. An adult may open a picture book at random and be so carried away by the quality of its illustrations that he must borrow or buy it; but it is the story that will captivate the child or leave him cold. All too often the language of picture books seems to exist for the sole purpose of justifying the binding together of a series of impressive pictures. This may be well worth doing; but why try to disguise the resulting product as a children's book? At its best, the picture book demonstrates the capacity of illustration to support and extend language, and of language to interpret illustration. It is easy to imagine that this will be achieved more commonly when author and artist are one and the same, but this is not necessarily so. Many fine artists, no doubt under the

delusion that the short, simple texts they have been asked to illustrate must be easy to produce, have tried writing their own texts
and failed. A master hand on both is needed, and producers of
outstanding texts for the two- to three-year-old seem to be in
shorter supply than able and sensitive artists.

When one person possesses a combination of talents, of course,
heights are sometimes reached. This is the case with John Burningham's Mr Gumpy, and Judith Kerr's superb story *The Tiger
who came to tea*. Here, picture and text seem to, and indeed have,
sprung from the one source. Near perfection of form is embellished
by clear and expressive illustrations. The pace is exactly right, the
resolution totally satisfying.

Sophie and her mother are having tea when there is a knock at
the door. Sophie answers it, and admits a 'big, furry, stripy tiger',
who plainly (but cheerfully) intends to join in their meal. Sophie is
enchanted and her mother admirably calm as the tiger eats his
way steadily through all the food on the table and, ultimately, all
the food in the house. Her mother evinces growing dismay as
excess piles upon excess, but Sophie remains enchanted. In the
end, the tiger departs, Daddy comes home, and there is nothing
else for it; they must go out to a café. This they do, Sophie consum-
ing a marvellous meal of 'sausages and chips and ice cream'. How
better could we leave her?

Pat Hutchins is an author-artist who has produced an impressive
number of picture books in little more than a decade. Her work is
for children, in the best possible way. Text and illustration are
mutually supportive, language simple and expressive, pictures a
celebration of clarity and colour.

Rosie's Walk has already become a classic. In twelve double
spreads, two single pages and thirty-two words, it describes Rosie
the hen's sober and purposeful journey through the farmyard '. . .
across the yard . . . around the pond . . . over the haycock . . . past
the mill . . .' At each point she is almost, but not quite, overtaken
by a fox who is hungrily pursuing her. He, poor animal, is himself
overtaken by a series of related catastrophes, unmentioned in the
text, but documented in the illustrations (he lunges at Rosie,
misses, and lands in the pond, the haycock collapses on top of him,

a bag of flour from the mill engulfs him . . .). Rosie stomps stolidly on, unseeing.

For fun, read *Rosie* to your two-year-old without mentioning the fox. It is, after all, a straightforward story. Repeat the performance at regular intervals (or as asked), and note the age at which he does notice the predatory fox and his ill-starred antics. You may be surprised, one way or the other!

The Wind Blew won the Kate Greenaway Medal for the year of its publication. For the young child, it is pure joy. Wide landscape pictures reveal, as the pages are turned, a growing succession of people pursuing their escaping possessions – all wrenched from their hands by the boisterous wind.

> *It plucked a hanky from a nose,*
> *And up and up and up it rose.*

The last few openings show a mad mixture of jostling people and flying paraphernalia, all of which is suddenly abandoned by the capricious gale. An even more muddled mix-up naturally results. Two- and three-year-olds will love finding and matching people and possessions in these vigorous and detailed pictures.

Good-Night, Owl! is even simpler, and is bound to succeed. It uses 'noise' words and the repetition so loved by the young, and has illustrations of extraordinary impact.

> *The woodpecker pecked, rat-a-tat! rat-a-tat!*
> *and Owl tried to sleep.*

> *The cuckoo called, cuckoo cuckoo,*
> *and Owl tried to sleep.*

Predictably, Owl, who likes to stay awake at night, finds the perfect way to retaliate . . .

Pat Hutchins speaks directly to small children. Her themes recognize their concerns, the limits of their understanding, their natural taste in humour. That her individual art style works so well to support and extend her stories is every child's good fortune.

Beatrix Potter's *The Tale of Peter Rabbit* naturally serves as the prototype for author-artist picture books. Peter is firmly instructed *not* to go into Mr McGregor's garden, does so, is pursued, almost caught, escapes without his 'blue jacket with brass buttons' and reaches the sanctuary of home – to incur his mother's disapproval and the punishment of no supper, and bed, with camomile tea. There is a breathlessness about Peter's adventures that is not often matched; certainly, no tangents or sub-plots interfere with its course and the tiny, now classic illustrations are a new delight and wonder to successive generations of children.

The 'well-read' two-and-a-half-year-old will be ready for this and several other Potter stories – and *Appley Dapply's Nursery Rhymes* is not to be missed at this stage, if not already known. This is a small gem of a book and can be read in three minutes: three minutes of enchantment. Could any three couplets, with facing illustrations, tell a more complete story than this?

> *Now who is this knocking*
> *at Cottontail's door?*
> *Tap tappit! Tap tappit!*
> *She's heard it before?*
>
> *And when she peeps out*
> *there is nobody there,*
> *But a present of carrots*
> *put down on the stair.*
>
> *Hark! I hear it again!*
> *Tap, tap, tappit! Tap tappit!*
> *Why – I really believe it's a*
> *little black rabbit!*

A word of caution about the indiscriminate use of Beatrix Potter at this time. There is a very wide language and interest range among the stories, and some of them have complex and sophisticated themes. *The Story of a Fierce Bad Rabbit* is certainly the shortest of the stories proper, but somehow lacks the cosy detail of the other tales. Before three-and-a-half, I would use only *Jeremy Fisher*, *Tom Kitten* and *Miss Moppet*, in addition to *Peter Rabbit* and *Appley Dapply* – and *Cecily Parsley's Nursery Rhymes*, which, while less distinguished in content, has the usual pictures. But do use them! Don't risk overlooking their capacity to captivate, and the opportunity they offer to familiarize the small child's ear with precise,

Victorian-parlour language ('I am affronted,' said Mrs Tabitha Twitchit.). As an antidote to the banalities of television utterance, Beatrix Potter's easily available little books should not go unused.

Repetition is a never-fail ingredient in stories for this age group, and Eve Rice's book *Sam Who Never Forgets* is classic in its progression. Sam, the zookeeper, loads his wagon and feeds bananas to the monkeys, fish to the seals, oats to the zebra . . . and then induces anxiety in the elephant's breast by departing. But all is well – he has merely gone off to re-load his wagon with golden hay because '. . . you do eat *such* a lot – so I've brought you a wagon all your own.' Sighs of satisfaction from the elephant, and two-year-old listener-looker! Eve Rice's earlier books established her expertise with small line drawing and muted colour; *Sam* demonstrates her capacity to use flat, primary colour to convey feeling and relate action.

It is comforting to have Eve Rice in the ranks of modern author-artists. Over-cleverness, and ignorance of the concerns and limitations of young children, are the twin banes of picture books for the rising-threes, and never does her work show evidence of these faults. Custodial figures, whether parents or zookeepers, are reliable, supportive and accepting. Situations are real, emotions basic and recognizable.

Niki Daly shows the same capacity for looking at the world from knee height in two small books, *Teddy's Ear* and *Ben's Gingerbread Man*. In the first title, Tim's loved-near-to-death teddy bear loses an ear, and has it restored by a Mum who is as warm and homely as he is typically two. In the second the dilemma is familiar: to eat or not to eat the gingerbread man made at nursery school? 'He's too special,' says Ben. But catastrophe strikes – Mum *sits* on the gingerbread man! – and Ben is desolate. Practical Mum instigates a baking session, and Ben comes to terms with reality.

> 'Where's your special gingerbread man?' asked Mum.
> 'In my tummy,' said Ben.
> 'Well, that's a safe place,' Mum laughed.

Both titles present small dramas of daily life; both will be requested again and again. Be sure to direct your small listener's attention to the endpapers of each. You will both relish them.

The six titles which together comprise the series 'Storytime' by Niki Daly (to which the above books both belong) illustrate a point made earlier about the uneven age-target which must some-times be recognized and considered, when such a series takes the eye. All six books are good-humoured, believable little tales, but only *Teddy's Ear* and *Ben's Gingerbread Man* present two-year-olds in action; the heroes and sole heroine of the other four titles are indubitably three or four, their concerns and activities reflecting their greater capacity. A small point, perhaps, but an important one, revealing the need to identify closely with your two-year-old's response to books. Fortunately you will be better at this than anyone else, by now; the experts may make all the learned noises they like, but you will *know*.

I feel that a word of caution is appropriate at this point. The modern conviction that the first few years of life are of prime importance for intellectual development sometimes produces a 'teaching' note in books for two-year-olds. Somehow, learning has become confused with fact-gathering. 'Let's teach the children the difference between up and down, black and white, fast and slow', many over-earnest educators seem now to be saying. And so we have a dreary progression of series called 'Learning about . . .' or 'What Do I See?' or 'How Does it Feel?'

I have never had any patience with these books; most of them are as dull as they are demeaning. They may have some usefulness for school beginners whose language development has been in-hibited by their backgrounds, but even here, the superior claims of simple, spirited stories to inform and inspire can be, and have been, demonstrated. And surely, the meaning that emerges from words used in context, and the lift that comes from language which in itself has life, colour and novelty, is what such children always need? I would give them only such language – beginning with nursery rhymes and jingles and proceeding by way of *The Owl and the Pussy-cat* to *Where the Wild Things Are*. To activate the brain, prod the emotions and stir the imagination every time!

Fortunately, some of the most inspired and able illustrators continue to see the point of giving attention to the old rhymes. One of them, Maureen Roffey, has invoked the aid of her husband,

Bernard Lodge, to supply additional verses for several traditional rhymes. The resulting books are brilliant examples of that unity of vision and intention that is, sometimes, achieved in a working partnership. I would introduce *The Grand Old Duke of York* between two and three (it will, on its own momentum, keep going for the rest of childhood – and could be used for cheerful sessions with a young baby – but Bernard Lodge's soft-hearted, silly old Duke speaks to a listening nearly three-year-old, I think).

The illustrations are masterly. The cover tells us that Maureen Roffey has also worked in children's television and advertising and has designed and produced children's toys and cards. No small talent, hers. The 'grandness' of the theme is well suited to the exclusive use of brilliant primary colours in the collage-style illustrations, with black (boots and busbies) and textured cloth (horse, barn and hen) relieving and supporting. The total effect is triumphant; but the text must be allotted at least half the distinction. Listen to it (the original ten thousand men have been eroded to a mere handful by this stage):

> *The grand old Duke of York,*
> *Had only twenty men;*
> *Fifteen marching through a farm,*
> *Were chased off by a hen.*
>
> *And two were lost in a barn,*
> *And two were lost in a sty,*
> *And the only soldier that was left,*
> *Ran off and waved goodbye.*

The Duke is grief-stricken. First he weeps, and then he throws away his sword and gun. But wait!

> *The grand old Duke of York,*
> *He heard a bugle sound.*
> *As he buckled on his sword and gun,*
> *His heart began to pound.*
>
> *He saw them in rows of five,*
> *He saw them in rows of ten,*
> *And they all lined up in front of him,*

Till he had ten thousand men.

Rousing stuff this, sung or said, and guaranteed to elicit the ultimate accolade: Read it again!

Hairy Maclary from Donaldson's Dairy succeeds before the cover is ever raised. In fact, the title itself will be repeated with relish, even if incorrectly, by the nearly three-year-old whose ear for the satisfactions of language is developing fast. A quite singular list of friends accompanies Hairy Maclary on his walk into town:

> *Schnitzel von Krumm*
> *with a very low tum,*
> *Bitzer Maloney*
> *all skinny and bony,*
> *Muffin Mclay*
> *like a bundle of hay,*
> *Bottomley Potts,*
> *covered in spots,*
> *Hercules Morse*
> *as big as a horse . . .*

All prove to be equally fainthearted when confronted by

> *SCARFACE CLAW*
> *the toughest Tom*
> *in*
> *town . . .*

with a verbal outcome which can only be described as delicious! Lynley Dodd has followed the original tale with three more, *Hairy Maclary's Bone*, *Hairy Maclary Scattercat* and *Hairy Maclary's Caterwaul Caper*. The now familiar characters will be welcomed with pleasure in each, their latest entanglements enjoyed to the full.

This is the Bear is a phenomenon that those readers who develop keen discrimination will come to recognize: an outstanding title which rears its head up from an 'easy reading' series which, while competently written and illustrated, is otherwise unexceptional. There is nothing unexceptional about *This is the Bear*. It has in full measure that quality of virtuosity which marks it out for success provided it is identified, asked for individually, and manages, itself, to escape the bonds of its series origin. Of course, it fulfils its role as a 'beginning reader' beautifully; and Helen Craig's sensitive and expressive pictures complement Sarah Hayes' terse and yet eloquent text precisely. But it is more than a 'reader'. The story is irresistible. 'The bear' – helpless in his plump, inanimate bearness – is pushed into the rubbish bin by 'the dog' – well-meaning but brainless – and ultimately rescued from the dump by 'the boy' who is resourceful, courageous and determined, in the best tradition of devoted bear-owners. All this is revealed in less than two hundred simple words, which, with the illustrations (in which 'asides' to the action appear in small balloons) contrive to create a tale in which drama, humour and pathos are nicely mixed.

The books I have described in this chapter are a varied collection: some sparkling, some quietly glowing, all inspiring or useful in their own way. One cannot possibly exaggerate the learning, of all kinds, which will proceed from their constant use with children between two and three – or older, for many of them will become staples. Those adults who are concerned to educate the very young may safely relax, if their children come to live with such books; to pore over them alone, and to hear them read aloud often. Information slips unnoticed into the mind, from such contact: varieties of people and places, shades of reaction to emergency, effects produced by action, new ways of looking at things, and people, new adjectives – their meanings self-apparent in context – all are encountered and absorbed when mind and senses are engaged in the fascinating game of story.

And this is real learning – learning that beds down and stays, because it happens joyfully, with nothing of duty associated. Anything missed the first time will be absorbed at second or third exposure as the young reader-listener grows in maturity: the best way to learn.

As her third birthday approaches, the world is opening up to the delectation and delight of the well-endowed child. She is less imprisoned by her own emotional responses than in the past. Increasingly, she is able to defer immediate gratification of her wishes; she starts to see that some things must be done before others can happen. She is on the way to becoming a reasonable being, and this factor will influence the sort of stories and books which she needs.

As children's spoken and understood language burgeons they enter a period which, for parents who themselves love books, is the best time of all for story sharing. Some of the best picture books of all time have been produced for the child over three. There is enchantment ahead.

Book List 3
Books to Use between Two and Three

Earlier books will still be in constant use, and some two-year-olds will be reaching forward into the next list.

'Ahhh!' said Stork Gerald Rose (Faber/Picturemacs paperback)
  Stork finds an egg and plans to eat it. However, he can't break the shell, so the other animals join in. Simple, brilliantly coloured pictures show how 'Hippopotamus rolled on it' . . . 'Lion bit it' . . . A surprise awaits them all. Economy of text, exact portrayal of action in illustration.

Alfie's Feet Shriley Hughes (Bodley Head/ Picture Lions paperback)
  This is the youngest Alfie book; and Alfie will become a friend, once met. Here, new gumboots are coveted, acquired, and worn to the park, a resigned but good-natured Dad in attendance. Alfie has fun stomping in puddles . . . but something seems to be wrong with the boots. Dad helps him change feet, and all is well. Nothing to it, really – but near three-year-olds identify rapturously. There is wry humour for the adults, too, in scenes of baby-and-toddler-encumbered mealtimes and shopping trips, with this author-artist's genius for invoking the messy cheerfulness which is all most of us can aspire to in the circumstances. Alfie and Annie Rose, with their likeable if unremarkable Mum and Dad are here to stay, I predict. (Further 'Alfie's' in Book Lists 5 and 6.)

*Appley Dapply's Nursery Rhymes Beatrix Potter (Warne)
  Other recommended titles by Beatrix Potter: **Cecily Parsley's Nursery Rhymes*, **The Story of Miss Moppet*, **The Tale of Mr*

Jeremy Fisher, * *The Tale of Peter Rabbit*, * *The Tale of Tom Kitten*.
Are You There, Bear?   Ron Maris   (Julia MacRae/Puffin paperback)

A circle of light from the torch shown on the title-page illu-
minates a succession of places in a bedroom where Bear *might* be
hiding. Before he is finally unearthed, other toys – Donkey,
Little Doll, Jack-in-the-Box – are revealed in likely spots, with
the family dog curled up in an armchair. Two-to-threes love
torches, and might explore their own dark bedroom, with help.
The toys are engaging, the device successful. (See also companion volume, *My Book*, below, in which the same bedroom is
revealed, with resident bear, donkey, the familiar cupboard,
and the family dog. Joseph, nearly three, and I, searched for the
cat from this title, unsuccessfully, in *Are You There, Bear?* Then:
'She's outside on the wall – remember?' said Joe. Obviously the
scenario had come to life as intended, for one small listener-
viewer.)

The Baby, *The Blanket*, *The Cupboard*, *The Dog*, *the Friend*,   *The
Rabbit*, *The School*, *The Snow*   John Burningham   (Cape)

Eight simple and satisfying little books which might be used a
year earlier, but will mean much more to the two-year-old.
Burningham's illustrations have delicate precision; these pictures
say even more than the deftly economical text.

* *Ben's Gingerbread Man* (and *Teddy's Ear*)   Niki Daly   (Walker)
Big Wheels   Anne Rockwell   (Hamish Hamilton)

The perfect book for the two- to three-year-old who is impressed
by large working vehicles but dazzled by two many details.
Front-end loaders, dump trucks, bulldozers and cement mixers
are brilliantly and simply pictured. Colours are primary, text
minimal. 'Big wheels are good. They help us every day.'

Cars   Anne Rockwell   (Hamish Hamilton)

Clear colourful pictures of cars old and new, big and small, 'on
six-lane motorways and on dusty country roads . . .' provide
compulsive viewing for very young motor enthusiasts. The
brief text seems mundane, but actually covers the material well.

The Day Dad Went for a Pint of Milk   Ron Clark, illus. Sue Geiber
(Hamish Hamilton)

Charley and his Dad set out one Sunday morning to buy a pint of milk. The trip takes a long time, because they find things to look at, and think of games to play on the way. All is seen from Charley's level, the mood is one of loving indulgence on a fine, no-work morning. Mum is waiting for them when they finally arrive home ('I thought I'd lost you'), and Charley is asleep on his father's shoulder. A slice of real two-year-old life, successfully presented in simple words and clear but delicate colour.

Dear Zoo   Rod Campbell   (Abelard-Schuman/Puffin paperback)
A flap book of distinction, with the theme of the title explored in eight double-spread, very stiff (even in the paperback) pages. Each presents, on the right-hand page, a door or a lid which, being opened, reveals an (unnamed) animal sent in answer to a request for a pet.

> So they sent me a . . .
> (Giraffe, behind a tall green door)
> He was too tall!
> I sent him back.

As a last try, the zoo dispatches a puppy . . . Satisfying stuff, in bright colour and excellent format.

The Elephant and the Bad Baby   Elfrida Vipont, illus. Raymond Briggs   (Hamish Hamilton/Puffin paperback)
This picture book has all the factors most likely to succeed with very young children: a racy text which calls for 'performance', an engaging and ever-enlarging list of characters, repetition, and two central figures who are bound to appeal. For good measure, it has Raymond Briggs's spirited illustrations, and a repeated jingle which will pass into the language:

> 'and they went rumpeta, rumpeta, rumpeta, all down the road.'

Feeding Babies   Chiyoko Nakatani   (Bodley Head/Puffin paperback)
This book is worth owning for its succession of animal pictures alone; Nakatani's work combines simple grace, precision and a masterly use of pastel colour. Eleven double spreads reveal ten animal mothers and one human feeding their babies. (The dog

on the title-page and mouse on final endpaper make thirteen all told.) Informative, and quietly beautiful.

Freight Train Donald Crews (Bodley Head)

One cannot imagine a more dramatic way of learning about colours and the way they merge. A freight train roars through the pages of this book, with 'Green cattle truck Blue coal truck Purple fruit van' and finally, magnificently 'a Black tender and a Black steam engine.' There is a feeling of movement, of gathering speed, mounting tension; and then the train is gone. A complete experience, accessible to the two-year-old.

*Good-Night, Owl! Pat Hutchins (Bodley Head/Puffin paperback)

*The Grand Old Duke of York Maureen Roffey and Bernard Lodge (Bodley Head/Magnet paperback)

Grandpa's Garden (also *Market Day, On the Road* and *What a Week!*) Sally Kilroy (Viking Kestrel)

Four tiny hard-covered books showing children engaged in the everyday occupations of energetic childhood, with warm and unfussy relations. Bright, perky pictures to match.

*Hairy Maclary from Donaldson's Dairy (also *Hairy Maclary's Bone* and *Hairy Maclary Scattercat*) Lynley Dodd (Spindlewood/Puffin paperback)

*Harry the Dirty Dog Gene Zion, illus. Margaret Bloy Graham (Bodley Head/Puffin paperback)

Katie and the Smallest Bear Ruth McCarthy, illus. Emilie Boon (Heinemann/Corgi paperback)

There is a rare quality about this book which, at surface level, is compounded of simple but satisfying story and bright but not garish illustrations. A more elusive component – wholesome innocence, perhaps – makes it very special indeed; and exactly right for two-to-threes.

Lucy & Tom's Day Shirley Hughes (Gollancz/Puffin paperback)

This is the 'youngest' of the well-known 'Lucy & Tom' books, and features an energetic little girl of about three, and her typically cherubic if irresponsible little brother of eighteen months or so. Their activities throughout the day are those of many small children: they 'help' Mum with the housework, go shopping, and create predictable domestic confusion with the greatest good cheer. Their world is seen from knee height in descerning detail by this observant and understanding author-artist. (See also Book List 4, page 118).

May We Sleep Here Tonight?   Tan Koide, illus. Yasuko Koide (Faber/Magnet paperback)

Three mice out on a hike get lost, find an empty house as night comes on, are joined by other small lost creatures – and receive a terrible shock when the owner, a BEAR, returns! No need; he is welcoming and gentle . . . The artwork is exquisite, the telling assured.

* *Mr Gumpy's Motor Car*
* *Mr Gumpy's Outing*   both by John Burningham   (Cape/Puffin paperback)

My Baby Brother Ned   Sumiko   (Heinemann)

A gentle, carefully detailed picture book which describes a small girl's involvement with, and attitude to, her baby brother. It might well serve as an example of how things should be, as both parents clearly understand their small daughter's need for reassurance of their continuing love for her, and Dad is just as involved as Mum in the everyday life of the family. The softly coloured pictures are clear and expressive, and provide plenty of extra detail for perusal. (See also *My Holiday*, Book List 5, page 184.)

My Book   Ron Maris   (Julia MacRae/Puffin paperback)

An engaging half-page device allows a small child to explore and re-explore the resources of this simple, but well-designed book – a companion to *Are You There, Bear?* (above). These excellent books should be used in combination; the overlap encourages much satisfying search and discovery.

Now We Can Go   Ann Jonas   (Julia MacRae)

Bright primary colours and clear, large text (thirty-three words in all) are used to show a small child, who might be either girl or boy, packing for a trip. On the first page we see a full toy box. By the time the youngster says 'Now we can go!' the entire contents have been transferred to a large bag, ready for departure. The endpapers show a wonderful mixture of toys against a

white background, encouraging the child to point and identify
– and enjoy.

Once: A Lullaby   B. P. Nichol, illus. Anita Lobel   (Julia MacRae)
This book has an almost mesmeric effect; appropriately, as it is
intended to assist the young into a state of sleepiness. A simple
verse is repeated no fewer than seventeen times, each stanza
introducing a different animal and its characteristic utterance.

> *Once I was a little cow,*
> *baby, cow, little cow.*
> *Once I was a little cow,*
> *Moo, I fell asleep.*

Any one of Anita Lobel's earthy and yet elegant pictures bears
prolonged scrutiny. Each is framed, and adheres strictly to the
overall plan: a small animal, with replica of itself as cuddly toy,
is seen in a flounced and ornamented bed, in a homely but well-
equipped bedroom. The relevant animal motif decorates the
wallpaper, an ornately framed family photograph hangs on the
wall, toys, books and a chamber pot litter the floor. Two tiny
pictures are arranged on either side of the centrally set text,
beneath the main illustration. The total effect is utterly satisfying. This should be an enduring book and will be especially
loved by two-to-threes (the 'Again!' brigade).

Peace at Last   Jill Murphy   (Macmillan/Papermac paperback)
This story has in full measure those essential but hard-to-find
qualities which make an enduring book: characters who appeal
immediately, action which is believable – however singular –
and a satisfying resolution. In this case, the pictures clinch the
deal; they depict a family of robust, good-humoured bears
against agreeable indoor and outdoor backdrops in warm colour
and clear outline. This is a book for all children – and will evoke
a rumble of sympathy from over-tired *human* parents.

*Rosie's Walk   Pat Hutchins   (Bodley Head/Puffin paperback)

*Sam Who Never Forgets   Eve Rice   (Bodley Head/Puffin paper-
back)

Sophie and Jack (and *Sophie and Jack Help Out* and *Sophie and Jack in
the Snow*)   Judy Taylor, illus. Susan Gantnor   (Bodley Head)

Susan Gantnor's greetings cards have already made famous the lumbering and lovable hippopotami which cavort in this engaging book and its sequels. There is an innocent, unpatronizing quality about these over-sized 'children' and their activities, and this, with the help of Judy Taylor's clipped comment, has been transferred neatly to the books.

In the first story the hippo family is seen on a picnic, and the children play hide-and-seek. In the second, their help in the garden produces surprising results, and in the third, they build a snow hippo. Colours are as bright and warm as a summer day, outlines clear and words minimal.

Springtime for Jeanne-Marie Françoise (Hodder & Stoughton)
Teddy at the Seaside (also *Teddy's Birthday*, *Teddy in the Garden* and *Teddy's First Christmas*) Amanda Davidson (Collins/Picture Lions paperback)

There can never be too many teddybears in the world and Teddy here has the solid qualities of the real article: he is stout, takes himself seriously, and expects to be treated as a member of the family. Although inanimate, he is certainly the centre of the action in these robustly coloured, detailed pictures – child-owner and family appear only as a brief leg or arm intruding from offstage. The comic-strip technique employed on many of the pages makes it possible for a very young child to 'read' by scanning from left to right, and down the page. The text is minimal. And don't miss the endpapers, which have style and tell a drawn-out story, continued from front to back.

Teddy Bear Coalman (also *Teddy Bear Baker* and *Teddy Bear Postman*) Phoebe and Selby Worthington (Viking Kestrel/Puffin paperback)

This appealing little bear-in-child's-clothing (engaging in grown-up occupations) first appeared on the literary scene almost fifty years ago. His appeal is perennial in all his guises; he is cheerful, industrious and quite without pretension. A day in his life makes fascinating listening and viewing, especially when accompanied by illustrations which are bright, detailed and colourful. (*Teddy Bear Gardener* by Phoebe and Joan Worthington preserves the tradition.)

This is the Bear   Sarah Hayes, illus. Helen Craig   (Walker)

Thomas Has a Bath   Gunilla Wolde   (Hodder & Stoughton)

> Thomas again (see *Thomas is Little*, Book List 2, page 59) cavorting in his bath. An occasional two-year-old develops an inexplicable fear of the bath. This book will help – but all small children will identify with Thomas and enjoy his cheerful activities.
>
> *Thomas and His Cat*, by the same author and publisher, is also just right for this age group. (Other 'Thomas' titles are given in Book List 4, p. 123)

The Tiger who came to tea   Judith Kerr   (Collins/Picture Lions paperback)

Tractors (and *Diggers* and *Special Engines*)   Paul Strickland (Methuen)

> Large vehicles – whether designed to dig, carry, move or rescue – are perennially seen as dramatic by young children. These competent, square, brightly illustrated little books present their subject matter graphically, and with a fair degree of accuracy. The text in each case makes little demand, contenting itself with a simple statement on each page, unconnected with what has gone before. Once acquired, the books will be used and enjoyed for several years.

The Train to Timbuctoo   Margaret Wise Brown, illus. Art Seiden (Golden Press, New York)

> An irresistible book. Repetition, train noises, a swaggering BIG train and a hardy little train, and a never-to-be-forgotten jingle:

> > Slam Bang grease the engine
> > throw out the throttle and give it the gun!

> Small children *play* this book over and over. (Out of print at the moment but the best Little Golden Books reappear at intervals.)

Two by Two   Betty Youngs   (Bodley Head)

> The domestic-cum-romantic quality of the Noah's Ark story is well served by this artist's lovingly embroidered pictures. Each double spread, in wide landscape format, has been sensitively planned; fingers will want to touch, wonderingly, while eyes explore the detail. The text is direct enough for two-year-olds, and has a lovely, lilting couplet to complete each page:

Those that walked,
And those that flew.

A love of language for its own sake begins with such experience.

The Very Busy Spider Eric Carle (Hamish Hamilton)

A simple, repetitive story, with an unusual feature: the 'silky thread' which this persistent spider uses to spin her web is raised from the page, so that small fingers can actually feel and trace it. On successive left-hand pages different farmyard animals suggest that the spider join them. 'Oink! Oink! grunted the pig. Want to roll in the mud?' The industrious spider does not answer; and between the chosen fence posts, her web grows and grows. Eric Carle's illustrations are, as ever, brilliantly coloured and well-designed. This is a satisfying book, certain to engage the attention of the two-year-old, who loves to touch as well as look and listen.

Walk Rabbit Walk Colin McNaughton and Elizabeth Attenborough, illus. Colin McNaughton (Heinemann/Pocket Puffin)

Rabbit, Fox, Bear, Cat, Pig and Donkey are all invited to Eagle's party, but only Rabbit decides to walk. The others, in various vehicles, suffer successive accidents in the best tradition of slapstick. The hare and the tortoise re-enacted! All is well in the end. Neat, detailed, expressive illustrations aid and abet this well-rounded story.

Who Sank the Boat? Pamela Allen (Hamish Hamilton/Hamish Hamilton paperback)

The ancient 'straw that broke the camel's back' theme is a familiar one in the world of picture books. Here, it emerges as fresh as a new day, with the characters – cow, donkey, sheep, pig and tiny little mouse – achieving truly individual status, and action pulsing along at breakneck speed. It is impossible to describe the virtuosity of the pictures, except to say that the animals manifest the most ridiculous attributes of humankind and yet remain animals. They are also lovable, unjudging and wonderfully innocent. The story is simple enough for a two-year-old, will come into its own again at 'early reading' time – and be savoured thereafter at any age.

The Wind Blew   Pat Hutchins   (Bodley Head/Puffin paperback)
Young Joe   Jan Ormerod   (Walker)

Joe can count one fish, two frogs . . . up to ten puppies . . . 'and one puppy chooses Joe for its very own'. This is my favourite of four 'Little Ones' from this sensitive and capable author-artist's pen. Our own near-three-year-old Joe copies book-Joe's actions throughout. What matter that 'ten' as a concept is beyond two-to-three-year-old comprehension? 'One, two, five, eight . . .' does as well, while learning proceeds; and the small animals enchant.

When I was Three . . .

5

When I was Three, I was hardly me

Your own self, indeed, at three; or nearly so. What isn't possible, when you can make yourself understood with real language, go upstairs one-foot-to-a-step, take yourself to the toilet and pedal your tricycle?

Babyhood is behind; gone with nappies and high chairs and potties. A year ago, the world beckoned and you wanted to run at it, but clung to parental skirts instead. Now you're *there* and it all whirls around you in dazzling colour and variety.

To the uninitiated, a roomful of pre-school children is just that; the only distinction is between babies who crawl and older children who walk. To the informed, of course, the difference between two- and three-year-olds is almost as marked as that between babies and toddlers.

The parents of just-turned-three-year-olds must be forgiven for assuming, with incredulous relief and joy, that they have now mastered the art of parenthood. This totally civilized being (their firstborn: the delusion does not endure beyond this point in the family) is clearly the result of their love and care through days of best-forgotten anguish. From here on, all will be well.

They are, of course, on the three-year-old plateau well known to veteran parents. Later, with subsequent children, they will treasure just-three tranquillity while they have it, merely praying that it will endure until rising-four, rather than shattering around their ears at three-and-a-half.

Three-year-old children, give or take a few months, do seem suddenly to be all-of-a-piece; to have reached a stage of equilibrium at which conformity begins to be attractive, when giving as well as taking is possible and co-operation positively enjoyed. People matter to them now; new friends are savoured; toys are even – joy unbounding to the adults in their lives! – *shared*. It is as if they suddenly stop, shouting 'No! No!' and flinging themselves on the floor (or whatever form their own particular brand of protest once assumed) and say, clear-eyed and interested, 'Yes, yes!'

The emerging capacity to cope with life physically accounts for much of the three-year-old's feeling of well-being, of course. Whereas two-year-olds run *into* things, almost as if they count on sofas and people to stop their blundering progress, the three-year-old moves with agility and dexterity. She can dodge, turn, and wheel about in mid-flight. Think what this means to her in terms of play possibilities! No wonder she feels better about the world and its intentions towards her. For the first time in her life she feels – she *knows* – that she is not totally dependent on others for personal needs. Less need for help means reduced interference. Choice is suddenly seen as a heady privilege.

But it is her accomplishment in the field of language which confers the greatest blessing upon the three-year-old's personality. It is as if 'perhaps' has just swum into her repertoire of response, rescuing her from 'yes' and 'no' – the two terrible extremes. Shades of meaning now start to be recognized and even, increasingly, expressed. All the wonderful modifying words – later, nearly, tomorrow, almost, wait, half, lend – emerge in blessed effectiveness! But don't imagine that merely knowing such words at two would have made any difference to social behaviour. Intellectual development, yes; but not her willingness to compromise. This comes slowly, and is only in its infancy at three; but it is discernible, if you look and listen carefully; the three-year-old has a new understanding of the world and her place in it.

The responsibility of catering for the book-and-language needs of this suddenly superior being would be sobering were it not so satisfying. Ironically, though, it is both easier and harder than before. Easier, because there is such a wealth of material available for children whose language and experience at last equip them for more complex and sophisticated stories, and harder because they will, inevitably and desirably, become more and more discriminating in their tastes.

They may also, suddenly, demand complete comprehensibility from books. Whereas before they expected to listen without understanding at least some of the time, now obscurities must be cleared up as they arise.

But there is a wide range of reaction in this area and it seems to relate less to intelligence and book-experience than to temperament. Some children have a precise, step-by-step approach to the gathering of information, and these children will seldom allow an unfamiliar word or concept to pass without explanation. 'What's a gander?' 'Why did she do that?' 'What does slumber mean?'

A prolonged session with such a child may well persuade you that the book in question is too advanced. The child, by contrast, may have thoroughly enjoyed the experience. Asking questions and receiving answers may be his or her idea of an enjoyable book session, even if you find the constant starting and stopping tiresome.

Another youngster of similar age and experience will hear the story out, unfathomables and all. This child may be simply less curious, but may also love the total effect of a story; may be prepared to take details on trust, for the experience of the whole. Our youngest child demonstrated this willingness in extreme form. When only two years old, she would sit in on family story-sessions intended for brothers and sisters of the eight-to-eleven age group, listening almost endlessly to language which must have been often incomprehensible. Even when it was time for the little ones' story, the choice was almost always made by someone else; Jo herself would listen intently and without comment or question, to anything anyone chose to read aloud.

Fascinating insights into the way language develops have been made in this century. The most interesting of these from our present point of view relate to the sort of environment in which children learn to use language best. Obviously, the more information we have on this score the better.

There is clear evidence that babies and small children profit from an environment in which language is used creatively, to examine ideas, relate occurrences and describe shades of meaning. Far from needing one-syllable words combined into simple sentences to expedite their learning, children need regular access to complex speech patterns if their own language is to develop richly. A truth that is still overlooked, or at least undervalued, is that what a child understands is actually much more important than what that child can express at a given time.

Meaning exists in the mind of the listener, not in the sound waves generated by speech, a fact that becomes obvious if one thinks of the uselessness of listening to someone speaking in an unknown foreign language. To keep the comparison going: think how easily children learn a new language if they go to live in a foreign country. Adults often try to learn words, phrases and rules of grammar beforehand. Children, less tense about the business, let the new language flow around and through them, pick up a reference here and there and are able quite quickly to use the local dialect, if not fluently, at least confidently. They don't need lessons on the agreement of adjectives and nouns, or the tense of verbs; they learn by listening, and relating what they hear to meaning, which resides in their minds. Nor do they fall into the fatal adult trap of translating word by word. Children know intuitively that meaning arises from language in full torrent.

So with their native language. Ideally, it flows around them, rich in content and imagery. From it, and using it, children construct their own view of the world. At no stage can they use, aloud, all the language they understand; their speech lags, inadequate to their insights. The danger lies in adult assumption that because young children can themselves produce only simple words and constructions, they must be spoken to only in speech which reflects this pattern. By this formula, many children are condemned to a meagre language diet, fare which makes a mockery of the rich, diverse equipment of their minds.

Attending to children's minds, then, is a profitable pursuit: good for them and rewarding for us. And reading aloud is one of the simplest and most enjoyable ways of providing this enrichment. Direct teaching is boring for children and tedious for adults. But stories, in exciting and varied profusion – that's a different matter! And the third birthday does seem to usher in a period of boundless opportunity in book sharing.

To begin with, it is a suitable time to introduce the first fairy stories. The three-year-old seems prepared to accept the 'other-world' quality of these earliest tales (the 'Beast Fables' they have been called, appropriately). I would suggest for a start *The Three Bears, Little Red Riding Hood, The Three Little Pigs, The Gingerbread Man* (hardly a beast, but of the same ilk), *The Three Billy Goats Gruff* and *The Little Red Hen*. These have in common features which render them suitable for the child whose contact with stories has so far been confined to simple, progressive narratives and straightforward cause-and-effect tales.

It is important to understand the difference between these stories and the more sophisticated tales, such as *Jack and the Beanstalk* and *Snow White*. The 'Beast Fables' help children to move into an imaginary world which is quite unlike their own, but whose qualities are universal. The characters are often in peril, but the child comes to know that they will emerge unharmed in the end if they are courageous and wise. The rules are rigid; the first two Little Pigs were eaten because they were foolish, the Gingerbread Man because he was, after all, a biscuit, and biscuits are meant to be eaten.

Motive in story is important, and must be comprehensible to the reader. The Billy Goats Gruff want to go up on the hillside to eat and grow fat. The Gingerbread Man runs away because running away is fun. Goldilocks uses the bears' furniture and tastes their porridge from motives of understandable curiosity. These are emotions and reactions which the three-year-old has experienced himself; there is a two-and-two-makes-four quality about these simple plots which is utterly satisfying.

By contrast, jealousy, revenge and obsession with wealth or power are not, as motives, accessible to the young child's understanding, and this lends a degree of horror to some of the more sophisticated tales. Even though in *The Three Little Pigs* the wolf proposes to make a meal of the perky little heroes (and does eat two of them in the best versions), it is in the nature of things that wolves will hunger after pigs — and the resultant contest has a rollicking quality which keeps horror at bay. The sustained hatred of the disguised queen for Snow White is a different proposition for the three-year-old; this is a human situation, in which penetrating evil is sensed but not understood; and the unknown and unknowable is always more horrifying than the revealed terror.

Not all three-year-olds will react with fear to the more complex tales, of course, but the possibility needs to be borne in mind. Fortunately most of them are much longer and more involved than the 'Beast Fables' and their use may well be deferred for other reasons. But some children will encounter them inevitably in story-sessions intended for older children. In this case, you will soon find out whether your child is resilient to their gross horrors or not! And we have ourselves to cope with; I have never been able to bring myself to read aloud any variant of that tale in which a giant, being duped by a visiting family of children which he proposes to kill, slits the throats of his own (eight?) children by mistake. We all have our own tolerance limit, and mine is reached just before this excess.

On the other hand, I am sure that my children met this tale in some form in their own reading; censorship has never been part of the contract for reading alone in our family. It was my own blood that curdled at this atrocity, not that of my robust sons and daughters.

The variety of forms in which the 'nursery tales' have been published, and their occurrence in collections and series at every level from 'mass market' up, makes choosing the appropriate version for the young child a baffling task. Fortunately the field has attracted a number of responsible and sensitive authors and artists, and the best versions tend to stay in print because they are successful.

Paul Galdone is the outstanding name to watch for, in single-picture-book treatment of these early traditional tales. His interpretations may somethimes surprise, but seldom offend, in my experience. From Galdone's big handsome *The Three Bears*, Goldilocks emerges, startlingly, as an individual, plain in person and brash in behaviour. In his similarly spectacular *The Three Billy Goats Gruff*, the dreaded troll has such presence and personality that one almost wishes he might avoid disaster. (One of my grandchildren at three-and-a-half always responded soberly, if not sadly to the troll's well-deserved end. For this child, Galdone's rascally imp was the hero of the piece, never the villain.)

As for the retellings themselves, always be sure, even with a recommended version, that you are happy with the details before reading it aloud. In the original version of *Little Red Riding Hood* (illustrated strikingly by William Stobbs in the Bodley Head edition), both small heroine and her grandmother are gobbled up irretrievably before the tale is out. If this outcome offends you, you will certainly pass on your unease to your young listener. It might be preferable to settle for a modified version in the first place – an illustration of the advisability of reading *every* story alone, always, before you use it with a child.

As with nursery rhymes, it is sensible to introduce different versions, buying some and borrowing others. An old friend in a new guise will be greeted enthusiastically, and comparisons made with interest. You will learn much about your child from his preferences if you watch and listen to him.

The 'original' tales (if such a description is valid) have been augmented over the years with others of the same type. Many have become classics, and keep turning up in new versions. Long may this tendency continue! A new author or artist contributes something of his own – a comment, an emphasis, a touch of humour in an unexpected place – and the tale is revitalized.

Such a tale is that of *The Enormous Turnip*. I remember loving it from my own childhood, when I met it in a school reader. This must have been a meticulous, blow-by-blow account, because I have always been faintly disapproving of the brevity of Helen Oxenbury's *The Great Big Enormous Turnip*, despite its obvious success with three-year-olds. And I will not have any version which does not end with, 'And they all had turnip soup for supper.' I add it, if it is not there.

An older, wordier version by Anita Hewett, illustrated by Margery Gill, *The Tale of the Turnip*, continues to be in successful use in our family. Here, the detail is rich and repetitive. 'The little old man the grandfather, the little old woman the grandmother, and the little girl the grandchild' together with their friends the little black cat and the little brown mouse, exert an almost hypnotic effect on reader and listener alike. Sadly, this excellent book is out of print; a casualty, no doubt, of the modern fetish for bright colour, as against the quieter charm of black and white. For Margery Gill's pictures, detailed and expressive as they are, are 'penny plain' rather than 'tuppence coloured'.

I suspect that many of the adults who demand full colour in the books they buy for very young children have not looked very closely at the way these children react to their books. To begin with, a picture book will stand or fall, in a young listener-looker's estimation, on the story and the way in which the illustrations support and interpret it. This bears repeating. *Story* comes first, with all its requirements: appropriate theme, well-shaped plot, characters who are sympathetic and who come alive, well-paced narrative which moves smoothly to a climax – and that elusive quality of 'wholeness' which is impossible to define but easy to recognize.

It is true that a five- or six-year-old who is introduced to books for the first time is more likely to be captured by bright red and blue than sober black and white. This, of course, proves only that an unsophisticated taste in any field demands impact rather than subtlety for its satisfaction (Disney rather than Sendak, shall we say). As experience widens, and taste refines, the graphic quality of a picture is tempered by other considerations. Sensitivity to line and form, and a feeling for relationship, develop unconsciously through access to the best picture books, but are unlikely to emerge spontaneously in youngsters whose experience of books has been limited. These children may need – almost certainly will need – wooing with eye-catching colour and slam-bang action if they are to be won over to books at all. The bright lights and loud noises of the modern world (even excluding the effects of television) have a lot to answer for in the impairment of children's sense of wonder.

You may feel, nonetheless, that your three-year-old is unlikely to be captivated by the apparent austerity of black and white. If this is the case, I suggest an experiment. Borrow or buy a copy of *Millions of Cats*, by Wanda Gag. In this lyrical and shapely tale a little old man sets out to walk over the sunny hills and down through the cool valleys in search of a cat, for which his wife longs. He finds, instead of one little cat:

Cats here, cats there,
Cats and kittens everywhere,
Hundreds of cats,
Thousands of cats,
Millions and billions and trillions of cats.

Text and picture are one here; they are experienced indivisibly. The lettering is hand-done, pictures and paragraphs expertly intertwined. One feels that colour would intrude. *Millions of Cats* is a unified experience; it has spoken directly to those children lucky enough to encounter it for fifty years, and will surely continue.

By all means make sure that your children have the joy of rich and varied colour in their books. But don't deny them the unique experience of word and illustration which are mutually supportive in the particular and rare way of some black-and-white picture books.

To return to traditional stories for the three-year-old.

Collections of stories are to be viewed with suspicion and examined with care. There is no substitute for reading at least one story from the book before a decision is made; and even then, you may find yourself using only two stories regularly from a volume which contains twenty. The main difficulty stems from a factor mentioned already in this chapter: the wide variation in emotional response required by different stories.

Some collections brashly set *The Gingerbread Man* and *Jack and the Beanstalk* cheek by jowl and try to reduce both to a lowest common denominator by the use of a uniform language and style. This practice usually suits neither, mainly because each requires separate, sensitive treatment, with different audiences in mind. Many children are ready for *The Gingerbread Man* at two-and-a-half; not many are ready for *Jack and the Beanstalk* in its best forms until six or over.

There is, fortunately, a collection which can be acquired with confidence for three-year-olds. Several stories will be usable from two onwards if their babyhood has been bookish, and several might be left until four, but Anne Rockwell's *The Three Bears and*

15 Other Stories will be in daily use for years. This book is actually the equivalent of sixteen picture books. No page is without an expressive colour picture, and every single story is usable. There is something especially satisfying about a book which can be taken along on any expedition – a picnic, a trip to the doctor, a long car or train journey – with a guarantee of stories for all moods and moments. *The Three Bears and 15 Other Stories* is a treasure trove; sturdy, not too big, thoroughly companionable.

A more recent, but equally useful collection, *The Helen Oxenbury Nursery Story Book* will give both pleasure and value for money at this time. The choice of stories – ten in all – is impeccable, and the cover a joy in itself. This artist's overriding quality has always seemed to me to be one of entwined delicacy and robustness; a quality which produces an unlikely but radiant suitability for young children and yet appeals to adults as well. Here the pictures are generous in size as well as number and the retellings sound. The whole is a superlative book.

There is another category which appeals to this age group and must be conceded a place in its literature. It consists of big, lavish volumes, of which Scarry's *What Do People Do All Day?* is probably the best-known example. (It is certainly one of the best of its kind.) The books themselves attract attention by reason of their sheer size, colour, and apparent value for money. They are full of pictures. Great double-page spreads reveal panoramic vistas of people (or animals dressed up as people) conducting their lives in every imaginable and unimaginable circumstance, against everyday and bizarre backgrounds; going places on land, on sea and in the air. The scurrying little characters are involved in activities and accidents at once wildly unlikely and comfortably familiar.

An upsurge in the production of such 'bumper' volumes occurred in the early to mid seventies, and related, I believe, to increasing media emphasis on the importance of the pre-school years for learning. Richard Scarry became a household name in the wake of mass-marketing methods which guaranteed his fame. Meanwhile many fine authors and artists working in the children's field went unnoticed by the greater public. Many parents who, for the best reasons, were anxious to introduce their pre-schoolers to books, had little or no knowledge of suitable titles or sources of information. But, almost without exception, they had heard of Richard Scarry!

Scarry began his career as an illustrator in the 1940s, later moving into writing. He can scarcely be termed, fairly, an author; his stories are at best commentaries on what is happening in his pictures. One suspects that this style speaks directly to children who are used to watching television and films regularly. There can be no doubt that Scarry's rounded, jolly little animal-humans, trotting or rushing about their cluttered world, attract and amuse them. Action is the keynote. Character and situation are stereotyped, and reaction is instant, predictable and absolute. Shock, dismay and grief abound and are invariably presented as funny to the viewer, regardless of their reality to the sufferer. In this, Scarry's work has much in common with the comic book, or filmstrip cartoon. For me, these books are all fairly shallow experiences – not usually damaging, but seldom inspiring either.

A more definite limitation of Richard Scarry's books should perhaps be mentioned. It is an important drawback, because it negates the very quality which supporters claim for his *Busy Busy World*, *The Great Big Air Book* and similar titles: that is, that they increase a child's knowledge of words and concepts and so expand his intelligence. I am not persuaded of this. These books set out to teach, and yet invoke a method which is hit-and-miss, if not slipshod. Facts seem to shoot from the page of a Scarry title like sparks from a wheel; there is seldom any unifying theme or purpose to lead to cohesion.

You may ask, 'Does this matter, if the youngster enjoys the book anyway?' and I would answer, 'No – unless *all* her books use these staccato, unconnected statements to describe character and action.' We all learn best by tying newly encountered information to an existing body of knowledge. Research shows that young minds need practice *not* in the random collection of facts, but in the discernment of common factors, the recognition of cause and effect, an understanding of action, development, result. Narrative prose – a story – engages the attention in a way which guarantees concentration and the making of connections between new material and old. The patterns laid down by the sensitive, rhythmical use of language are lasting ones. Children respond later to words which flow, language which brings image to the eye and music to the ear; language which ensures that information is absorbed, apparently without effort.

These large impressive books are valuable if kept in their place: as supports to the mainstream of literature for the three-to-sevens, the central current of which is *story*. Certainly, they can widen a child's knowledge of things, activities and places, but their content is unlikely to linger in the mind long after the book itself is forgotten, as a story with real characters will do.

'What about Dr Seuss?' is a question which hangs in the air at this point. Is it time for *The Cat in the Hat* and *Horton Hatches the Egg?* Once again, discrimination is needed.

The 'Beginner Books' are a phenomenon. Never before has a series aimed directly at very young children so caught the attention of the average parent. Beginning with *The Cat in the Hat* in 1957, 'Beginner Books' quickly multiplied. New and different authors were recruited to keep the image alive, and they achieved distinction in their own right. Stan and Jan Berenstain, P. D. Eastman, Syd Hoff and others have all played their part in the establishment of a series which is still, thirty years later, loosely called the Dr Seuss Books. If you had lived through the real 'Beginner Book' era as the parent of a young child, you would remember the near fervour which greeted the appearance of each new title. Some families owned every single volume – numbering more than fifty – and used no other books at all. The number available is still bewildering.When to start? Which to use? How to judge?

As before, the formula is the same; every title in the series must be considered separately. Several are brilliant, some are good, many are mediocre and a few are downright poor. Again, as in the Beatrix Potter books, the level of required understanding varies dramatically from story to story. There is no substitute for careful pre-reading of each title, with your own child's level of understanding and taste at the forefront of your mind.

And the best in my opinion? Well, all those years ago, my youngest children loved *Are You My Mother?*, *One Fish, Two Fish,*

Red Fish, Blue Fish, A Big Ball of String and *The Digging-est Dog* –
and our son Simon became positively addicted to *Green Eggs and
Ham*, which I personally consider one of the silliest books every
written. (I was obliged to continue reading it aloud through clenched teeth when everyone else finally rebelled. Years later I find
that its fatuous sentiments are still there, in all their absurd inanity,
to torment me if my eye happens to fall upon the wretched book
on shelf or in list.) Another loved title, *Robert the Rose Horse*, has
been inexplicably out of print for some years. Both this excellent
book and *A Fish Out of Water* – an abiding favourite in my family –
are more suitable for children over four, and I have included the
latter title in Book List 5.

There, also, you will find mention of several individual titles
written by Dr Seuss himself, which should not be missed at about
school-entry stage.

All the 'Beginner Books', of course, make good 'read-alone'
material once children launch themselves upon the serious business
of 'gleaning meaning from print'. At this time *The Cat in the Hat*
and all his clownish colleagues with their jaunty and repetitive
texts and funny (if sometimes vulgar) illustrations, ensure immediate attention. And *Dr Seuss's ABC*, already mentioned in Chapter 3,
will remain a staple throughout toddlerhood and into early school
years, if acquired early.

In the first edition of *Babies Need Books*, I deferred mention of
poetry beyond nursery-rhyme stage, to the last chapter. In the
intervening years, I have become more convinced than ever that
language, in all its resource and vitality, must become part of
children's very beings long before 'official' education begins, if
they are to use their minds and emotions confidently, flexibly and
imaginatively. My continuing observation of young children per-
suades me that poetry probably gives the richest return of all in
these stakes; but suggests also, that this area of children's access
to language is likely to be the most neglected of all.

There is, of course, a sort of 'chicken-and-egg' pattern in evidence; most parents, having not themselves experienced the mental
and emotional stimulation of rhythm and rhyme – 'the best words
in the best order' – early in life, are likely to be awkward with

poetry, if not actually derisive of its relevance to life. Sadly, these attitudes take root by early adolescence in all but a few children. Poetry comes to be seen as affected; effeminate, in the old, demeaning sense; even hypocritical, or bogus.

No such danger with the three-year-old! Try reading him

> Someone came knocking
> At my wee small door;
> Someone came knocking,
> I'm sure – sure – sure;
> I listened, I opened,
> I looked to left and right,
> But nought there was a-stirring
> In the still, dark night . . .

and watch his eyes grow round with the wonder, the heartfelt mystery of Walter de la Mare's evocative words. (from 'Someone' by Walter de la Mare.)

Try

> The pickety fence
> The pickety fence
> Give it a lick it's
> The pickety fence
> Give it a lick it's
> A clickety fence
> Give it a lick it's
> A lickety fence . . .

and see if the magical beat of David McCord's words doesn't elicit a grin, at least; a delighted shout, in all likelihood – 'Read it again!' (from 'The Pickety Fence' by David McCord.)

I believe that this experience is such a thing of the ear and the nerve ends that it should, much of the time, be unaccompanied by illustration. I will concede that poetry and colourful pictures can co-exist to produce an attractive and successful book; indeed, I have included examples of such happy collaboration in my lists. But experience with real children over a long period of time has reinforced this belief. A poem which demands attention from the ear only, purposely allowing the 'inward eye' to operate, allows the imagination fuller rein. And what lively, passionate imaginations children have!

When my own children were small, I began collecting poems which 'worked' for us as a family. Handwritten, they came to be housed in an old folder which ultimately burst at the spine. At this point, I divided them into 'younger' and 'older' selections and kept right on. (A large family, in which the oldest grandchild is a bare eight years junior to the youngest child, gives a generous time-span for this sort of exercise.) Several years ago, Hodder and Stoughton published these two little books, now called *For Me, Me, Me* and *I Will Build You a House*. Considerately, my editor deferred to my preference for a simple 'Pooh Bear' format, with small line drawings only.

I have found that *For Me, Me, Me* is ideal for using with three-year-olds; but then, of course, the poems are those that my children and grandchildren have loved. I hope you will try them with your own three-year-old; or better still, use those that you both like as a basis for *your* personal collection.

It is understandable that parents should feel that books about 'real' things matter. Life is a serious business, they reason; the sooner the child starts to collect facts, the better. This is true, as far as it goes, but it stops short of a profound truth. In the early years, facts and feelings are not clearly differentiated – and feelings endure longer than facts, at any age. There is a much greater chance that a fact will take root in the mind if it comes in on the wings of a feeling, a stirring of the emotions as well as the intellect.

Similarly, an interest in a subject that is kindled by an imaginative story will demand its own explanation later. As an example, let's look at Don Freeman's *A Rainbow of My Own*:

> Today I saw a rainbow. It was so beautiful that I
>   wanted to catch it for my very own. I put on
>   my raincoat and hat and ran outdoors.
> Fast as the wind I ran
> But when I came to where the rainbow should
>   have been, it wasn't there.

The illustrations show a dark, smudgy-grey sky against which the rainbow – and the small boy's bright yellow raincoat and hat – stand out in bright relief. Rapturous attention is guaranteed. By all means try to *explain* the rainbow phenomenon to your small son or daughter if you want to. Children 'catch' enthusiasms; we should all try to let them share ours. But don't expect the details to take root in their minds as the feeling of this story will in their senses. Why worry? Not knowing about the origin of rainbows until ten or twelve won't hurt them, and the magic and wonder of such a story will give the explanation, when it comes, an impact that will help it to stick.

One last word before we move on to the big world of the sophisticated over-fours. The factor which must guide you before all others is your own child's reaction to different books – and this may astonish you. It is quite common for a youngster to become almost addicted to one particular title, and to insist upon its repetition day after day, night after night, when all available readers-aloud have passed the point of no return in boredom. Clearly, such a title (and it may not even be a 'good book' by the experts' judgement) is meeting a need which will probably remain undiagnosed. All you can do, I think, is to grit your teeth and keep reading. By all means suggest – and produce – other seductive volumes, but on no account criticize the adored book. It has probably become part of him by this time, and your disapproval could be experienced as a personal betrayal. Anything as intense as this devotion *has* to be seen as important, even if the need, and its fulfilment, are not understood at all. (No use asking the youngster. *He* won't know in his head; only in his bones and all his fibres.)

And be prepared for (but don't jump to conclusions about) *real* individual differences in children. Many three-year-olds are impassioned by fire engines, earth-moving machinery, animals, or a host of other preferences. It is sensible to try to find titles which will satisfy these interests, but dangerous to cast a child in any particular mould. This happens more often to boys, I suspect. The casual onlooker might well have been convinced that Anthony, at just over three, would prefer his *Big Book of Machines* to any other title; his preoccupation with motorized lawn-mowers was intense. They would have been wrong, however. *Sally's Secret; Farmer Barnes*

Buys a Pig; Happy Birthday, Sam; The Trouble with Jack; The Very Little Girl; all the Jeanne-Marie books; all the tales from *The Three Bears and 15 Other Stories* – he requested these and countless other, very different stories constantly.

An apparent fixation with a particular topic (rather than a particular title) makes it important that you offer a wide selection, taking in both reality and fantasy, and including traditionally male and female topics, for children of both sexes. It is impossible to avoid the suspicion that many supposed preoccupations are cemented at an early age by well-meaning but short-sighted parents. Let's not risk turning all our poets into scientists – or vice versa.

You needn't worry, if your policy so far has been an open one. You will in all probability be panting behind, rather than leading, your youngster as the fourth birthday approaches.

Book List 4
Books to Use between Three and Four

Many of the books from earlier lists will still be loved, and some children will be moving on to stories from the next, and last section (Book List 5, page 162).

Alfie Gets in First Shirley Hughes (Bodley Head/Picture Lions paperback)

Alfie is every three-year-old, running ahead of Mum, intent upon reaching home first. This he does, easily; after all, Mum is encumbered with Annie Rose in her pushchair, as well as the shopping. It is when Alfie contrives to shut himself (*and* Mum's basket containing the key) inside that the trouble starts. Everyone helps on the outside – neighbours, milkman, window-cleaner – but in the end it is Alfie himself, alone on the inside, who takes action. The final double spread is utterly engaging

Then the window-cleaner came down from his ladder, and he and the milkman and Mrs MacNally's Maureen and Mrs MacNally and Annie Rose and Mum and Alfie all went into the kitchen and had tea together.

And there they are. Warmth, concern, humour and masterly use of pen and brush have together created a book which will endure.

An Evening at Alfie's has the same cast in another domestic drama. Mum and Dad have gone out for the evening leaving Alfie and Annie Rose in the competent hands of Mrs MacNally's Maureen. All goes well, until a burst pipe fractures everybody's

peace, and necessitates the summoning of first Mrs MacNally
and then, as the situation worsens, Mr MacNally. Good will and
hard work restore order, with Alfie clearly enjoying an unexpected evening's fun. This is real life, between the covers of a
book, superbly accomplished in word and picture.

Ambo and the Little Elephant
A Donkey's Tale
An Elephant's Tale   all by Bunshi Iguchi   (Dent)
I have bracketed these three satisfying, beautifully presented
stories together, as they have much in common; and yet each is
quite individual. A warm and gentle care for all life, human and
animal, characterizes the work of this famous Japanese author-
artist. Each of his double spreads is filled with visual riches. The
colours glow, and yet are muted; the softly outlined figures
come to life against landscapes which are filled with light and
colour. Children should, I believe, encounter a wide range of
art styles, early in life. Here is an opportunity for exposure to a
style which, in its technique and sensitivity, will extend their
experience, as well as reward and inform. Each story is uncomplicated and well paced; and the books themselves with their
square, generous format, are a joy to handle.

Andrew's Bath   David McPhail   (Blackie)
Picture books in which children interact with animals (or monsters, or ghosts) who just might have been imaginary, are now
quite common; doubtless because they serve a need, in reflecting
or even suggesting children's own fantasy games. Here, Andrew
goes upstairs to bath himself for the very first time, equipped
with 'all his favourite toys and books'. His parents' consternation
at the resulting noise – and Andrew's shouted reports – are
more than justified. A frog, a hippopotamus, an alligator, a lion
and an elephant have joined the watery fun. The pictures are
quietly expressive.

The Bear's Toothache   David McPhail   (Magnet paperback)
The bear, discovered outside the boy's window one night, is
huge, lumbering and in pain. The boy himself is sympathetic
and helpful. An engaging fantasy effectively complemented by
its realistic pictures, in interesting purplish tones.

Anno's Counting Book Mitsumasa Anno (Bodley Head/Picture-macs paperback)

In this elegant and unusual book, the same wide landscape is seen at twelve successive openings. In the beginning, the scene is empty except for a winding river. Gradually it develops. Through different seasons and periods of time a growing number of people and animals inhabit a landscape which becomes more and more complex. Each opening is built around a number, from 0 to 12. Each has a balanced elegance, its intricate pattern subtly conveying mathematical concepts and relationships. An absorbing book.

Are we Nearly There? Louis Baum, illus. Paddy Bouma (Bodley Head)

Watercolour illustrations of very fine quality indeed extend and grace a text which is confined almost entirely to conversation between a father and his small son in this successful book. They are on their way home from a day's outing by train. Only on the last page do we realize that the young man is delivering the child to his mother, rather than returning with him. There is sadness but no sentimentality in the picture of the father waving as he goes. 'Goodbye, Simon.' 'Goodbye, Dad.' 'See you soon . . .' Simon himself is all confidence and tired pleasure, red balloon trailing. Almost all families are touched by separation or divorce these days. This sensitive documentation of a happy day in the life of a child and his father will speak to some children directly, and draw others into the circle. This quality, in a book which stands alone as a 'good read' without it, makes it memorable.

*Are You My Mother? P. D. Eastman (Collins, Beginner Books)

First published in 1960, this book has been in constant favour with small children ever since. While it is certainly simple enough for two-year-olds its humour appeals to the three-year-old's greater sense of the ridiculous. A little bird, having hatched during its mother's absence, sets off to find her, asking inappropriate animals and machines in turn, 'Are you my mother?' The pictures, as usual in this series, are exuberant and absurd rather than sensitive. The story carries the day.

A Bag Full of Pups Dick Gackenbach (Viking/Puffin paperback)

An age-old formula is here put to pertinent use. The first page reveals old Mr Mullin bearing an enormous bag which is erupting with puppies – twelve in all, every one up for offers. First a farmer and then a succession of other potential owners (from the bizarre to the average) appear. Slowly, the group diminishes, until one small seemingly unwanted pup remains. Predictably, along comes a little boy . . . The pictures are explicit and animated, the puppies deliciously perky. An irresistible tale, deftly handled.

Belinda's Balloon Emilie Boon (Heinemann/Corgi paperback)

Lucy Bear loves wheeling baby Belinda in her pram in the park, and Belinda loves the balloon Lucy buys for her. When disaster strikes, and the balloon bears the baby aloft, Lucy displays both courage and imagination in a successful rescue attempt. The bears are hearty and wholesome, depicted with style by an artist whose work is direct, uncluttered, and buoyant.

Benny Bakes a Cake Eve Rice (Bodley Head/Picture Lions paperback)

Birthday celebrations are of prime interest to small children and the cake, complete with candles, is the central feature. Benny helps Mum make and decorate a magnificent cake – and is devastated when Ralph, the dog, wrecks their efforts. A phone call to Dad works the miracle . . . All is brought to life in Eve Rice's softly coloured, orderly pictures.

**A Big Ball of String* Marion Holland (Collins, Beginner Books)

Caps for Sale Esphyr Slobodkina (World's Work)

Another classic, in print since 1957 (but the story is much, much, older). This book illustrates the picture-book recipe to perfection: simple but well-rounded plot, interesting characters, a satisfying climax – the whole supported by pictures which tell the story and are themselves eloquent. A pedlar has his wares (tiers of caps, which he carries on his head) stolen by a tree-full of monkeys. He gets them back, by chance rather than good management. This story works, always, even with reluctant listeners.

Cars and Trucks and Things that Go   Richard Scarry   (Collins)
Twenty-three large double spreads – taking in both sets of end-papers – will provide young two- and four-wheel enthusiasts with extended opportunities for intent perusal and identification. The text is almost impossible to read aloud, but opportunities exist for parents to share in the discovery, speculation and sheer fun of it all. Nonsensical vehicles (a hot-dog car which is clearly a modified sausage, and a toothpaste car that's a made-over tube) alternate with dazing varieties of truck, car, bus, tank, bike, ferry and tractor. A family of cheerful pigs makes its way unscathed through a succession of spectacular pile-ups, and Officer Flossy on her bicycle pursues Dingo Dog through the whole book to bag him at last on the final page. Rousing stuff; I'd tell your three-year-old that this book is for 'looking at' and hope for some peace.

* *The Cat in the Hat*   Dr Seuss   (Collins, Beginner Books)

The Christmas Book   Dick Bruna   (Methuen)
Simplicity itself, and utterly engaging, is this very first version of the Christmas story:

> On a dark night long ago, and in a far country, some shepherds were keeping watch over their sheep. Suddenly a bright light shone on them.

This book is notable in its field. The subject is handled sensitively but not sentimentally, and the illustrations have remarkable feeling, as well as Bruna's usual clarity.

Corduroy   Don Freeman   (Viking Press, New York/Puffin paperback)
The story of an engaging toyshop bear who is longing to be bought. As time goes by, he starts to give up hope. But a litltle girl has her eye on him, and all is well in the end. Corduroy must be one of the most lovable of all lovable bears. The illustrations do him justice; in quiet colour, they are clear and expressive. (This notable book is out of print in England, but still flourishes in its homeland, America. I cannot believe that it will not be seen again, and so include it. Try the library, meanwhile.)

The Cow Who Fell in the Canal   Phyllis Krasilovsky, illus. Peter Spier   (World's Work/Puffin paperback)

Hendrika is bored and unhappy, until the day she falls in the canal, stumbles on to a raft, and floats gently down to the town. Peter Spier's double-spread pictures of Dutch town nd countryside are panoramic, meticulously detailed and utterly absorbing. Continuously in print since 1957, this splendid book must be regarded as a classic.

Daisy and the Washing Machine Tony Bradman, illus. Priscilla Lamont (Methuen)

This book is a small gem which might well pass unnoticed, concealed as it is in a group of 'Daisy Tales', and easily eclipsing its companions. Daisy helps Dad do the washing and, unbeknownst to him, stuffs her rag doll in at the last moment. The results are predictable, Dad is cross 'but not for long' . . . and the whole rings true as a glimpse of genuine family life. The pictures extend the text without swamping it. Priscilla Lamont's people, great and small, come alive.

* *The Digging-est Dog* Al Perkins, illus. Eric Gurney (Collins, Beginner Books)

Dudley Goes Flying (also *Dudley and the Monster*, *Dudley and the Strawberry Shake* and *Dudley in the Snow*) Judy Taylor, illus. Peter Cross (Walker)

The illustrations in these small books are exquisite, and will encourage scrutiny, as the detail is fascinating. Dudley is an engaging dormouse whose spirited sorties into the world of the countryside are not always as rewarding as he would wish; but will certainly entertain child readers.

Everybody Said No! Sheila Lavelle, illus. Nita Sowter (A. & C. Black)

An uproarious variant of *The Little Red Hen*. Mrs Mudd buys an apple tree and asks her large, cheerful family to help her plant it . . . water it . . . pick the apples. 'But everybody said no!' Nita Sowter's illustrations sparkle. A delightful book.

Farm Alphabet Book Jane Miller (Dent)

This book makes a visual impact, with its black pages, clear white print and eloquent photographs of farm life. A companion volume to the *Farm Counting Book* (see Book List 2, page 56), it is somewhat more complex in nature: a short but informative text supports pictures that are structurally more sophisticated than those in the earlier book. Three- to four-year-olds will pore over the subtly coloured pictures, finding more to enchant and inform at each encounter. Both upper-and lower-case letters are well placed for easy identification, and a narrow white line ties all together visually.

The Fat Cat Jack Kent   (Hamish Hamilton/Puffin paperback)
A Danish folk tale concerning a cat who eats an astonishing list of people and animals before his moment of disaster arrives. The text is jaunty and repetitive and the pictures full of fun and action, in this excellent retelling.

**For Me, Me, Me* Dorothy Butler (ed.), illus. Megan Gressor (Hodder & Stoughton)

The Fox went out on a chilly night   illus. Peter Spier   (World's Work/ Puffin paperback)
A superb rendering of this irresistible old song. One is at all times on the side of the fox and his 'little ones, eight, nine, ten,' and surely *everyone* knows the tune! (It is given in the back, in case.) The illustrations show authentic inside and outside scenes in an old New England setting. Every viewing reveals another fascinating detail, in this lasting volume.

Traditional stories by Paul Galdone   (World's Work)
The Gingerbread Boy
The Little Red Hen
Little Red Riding Hood
* *The Three Bears*
* *The Three Billy Goats Gruff*
The Three Little Pigs
The above stories are all suitable for use with three- to four-year-olds. The books themselves are alike only in their excellence; Paul Galdone contrives to give each a character of its own, while yet preserving its age-old flavour in the retelling. Colour is clear and lines are flowing in these expansive books. All will be handled with love and read again and again.

Grandma Goes Shopping Ronda and David Armitage   (Deutsch/ Puffin paperback)

> On Friday Grandma went shopping
> and she bought an amiable alligator

– and there she is, plodding smugly along with her unlikely purchase on a lead. Before long her mounting pile of shopping includes some startlingly inappropriate items, and Grandma herself, in newly acquired candy-striped jumpsuit, is bowling along on a bicycle built for two with a variegated vicuna riding tandem! Repetitive nonsense in cheerful colour, against a background which offers endless opportunity for profitable perusal – with an entertaining twist before the reassuring 'home to tea' finale.

The Great Big Enormous Turnip   Helen Oxenbury   (Heinemann/ Piccolo paperback)

Gwenda Turner's Playbook   Gwenda Turner   (Viking Kestrel)
Exactly fifty words succeed in conveying the wealth of diverse activities and games that children enjoy in a good modern nursery school. The pictures are the real joy, and they will be perused, scanned, examined, lingered over and talked about endlessly by the youngster who either looks forward to, or already experiences inclusion in such a group. This artist's children are shrewdly observed, honestly and warmly presented. 'We have lots of fun,' affirms the last page, beneath a 'class photo' line-up in which the observant may identify every child seen earlier in sand-pit, on swing or at the carpentry bench.

The Helen Oxenbury Nursery Story Book   Helen Oxenbury (Heinemann)

How St Francis Tamed the Wolf   Elizabeth and Gerald Rose (Bodley Head)
There is no more engaging saint than Francis, who loved all animals, and here he has been guaranteed endurance in the affections of modern children. This St Francis is robust and humorous. He tells Brother Wolf how wrong it is to eat people, and thoroughly enjoys the feast which celebrates his victory of kindness over violence. This old story is one to grow on, and is here very well served, both by text and picture.

The Lazy Bear   Brian Wildsmith   (Oxford/Oxford paperback)

Wildsmith's use of colour is incomparable. His picture books are extravaganzas, but are balanced by the earthiness of his subject matter, and the warmth and humour of his characters. Here, Bear (who is lazy but lovable) finds a trolley and contrives to have all the fun of riding in it while his friends (who are mild but not meek) do all the work of pushing. Their ultimate retaliation is effective, without being spiteful. A heartening story, made memorable by magnificent illustrations.

A Lion in the Meadow Margaret Mahy, illus. Jenny Williams (Dent/Puffin paperback)

The new edition of this already famous book ensures its inclusion among picture books which will survive, I believe. The author has given the story a new, less abrupt ending; the final double spread shows small boy, mother and lion in a bedtime 'read-aloud' scene which fuses the ordinary and the fabulous facets of the narrative perfectly. The new illustrations provide a feast of colour and detail.

*Little Red Riding Hood illus. William Stobbs (Bodley Head)

Lucy & Tom's Day

Lucy & Tom go to School

Lucy & Tom at the Seaside

Lucy & Tom's Christmas

Lucy & Tom's a.b.c all by Shirley Hughes (Gollancz/Puffin paperback)

The concerns of small children are universal. This likeable and natural pair make their way through five books without ageing noticeably; they play, protest, explore their world – from the delights of a day's visit to the sea, to the excited preparation for Christmas Day, and the joys and rigours of its actual arrival – with the zest of early childhood. In the second book, Lucy starts school and Tom goes to nursery school. The alphabet book, far from any sober intention to teach, provides a fascinating insight into the children's lives, with 'G for Granny and Grandpa, two other very important people', 'm' for 'moon, the most magic light of all' – in each case providing the viewer with a wealth of detail from which to identify and savour additional objects. Information and fun, in equal proportions, with that warmth and humour one has come to expect from this outstanding author-artist, abound in all five books.

Millions of Cats Wanda Gag (Faber/Puffin paperback)

Mog the Forgetful Cat (also *Mog and the Baby*, *Mog in the Dark* and *Mog's Christmas*) Judith Kerr (Collins/Picture Lions paperback)

Mog exasperates her human family. She cannot remember how to get back into the house through the cat-flap they have considerately made her and is forever miaowing outside the window. But in the end she helps to catch a burglar! This artist's incomparably clear, colourful illustrations tell the story exactly. A most successful book, as are the sequels.

The Most Amazing Hide-and-Seek Alphabet Book Robert Crowther (Viking Kestrel)

This is a unique book; certainly a 'pop-up', but with features which remove it from the pure 'action and fun' category of most such books. Each landscape page reveals three big, lower-case letters in alphabetical succession: a, b and c on the left page, d, e and f on the right, and so on. But what letters! Pull the tag at 'f' and up jumps a frog, uncovering also the printed word 'frog'. The top half of 'e' turns down as a flap, revealing an elephant who waves his trunk cheerfully – and thus to 'z', with inevitable zebra. All are banished at will by manipulation of the flap or tag. Each page is headed with both upper- and lower-case letters, and the design of the whole is impeccable. A notable book, this.

Mr Bear's Chair Thomas Graham (Hamish Hamilton)

Mr and Mrs Bear are a lumbering and loving pair, depicted by this truly individual author-artist in an uncluttered, richly hued environment which is backwoods, early American, rather than peasant European. At breakfast Mrs Bear's chair collapses underneath her, and she falls down . . . 'CRASH!' 'Just you wait,' says practical, caring Mr Bear. (He has already made the pancakes his wife has been eating with such enjoyment.) 'I'll have a surprise for you by supper.' Eight following vistas show him trudging off to the meadow, axe on shoulder and tool-box in hand, felling an old walnut tree and systematically making a new chair. Details of both picture and text are clear and correct. Old-fashioned tools whose functions can be observed and followed are shown in close-up: 'Then he shaved, and planed and drilled, and chiselled.' Mrs Bear is ecstatic; a sensitively designed double spread reveals her embracing her husband, while the beautifully proportioned new chair stands eloquently alone on the opposite page. But all is not to be resolved so easily. Mrs Bear has prepared a turkey dinner in celebration, but when the delighted Mr Bear sits down . . . The last page shows him again, axe on shoulder and tools in hand, making for the woods. This is a totally satisfying book: gently humorous, warm and informative.

My Brother Sean Petronella Breinburg, illus. Errol Lloyd (Bodley Head/Puffin paperback)

Sean is every three-year-old starting playschool. He wants to go and he hates the idea, simultaneously. In these brilliant, simple, vivid illustrations, and the sparse text, his agony and his joy come across. A superb book. The sequels, *Doctor Sean and Sean's Red Bike* (Bodley Head), show the small hero in a series of situations which typify the everyday life of his age group.

Old Macdonald Had a Farm Rowan Barnes-Murphy (Hutchinson)

Almost any age group would love this engaging 'flap' book, but the humour will appeal strongly to three-year-olds. A rather truncated version of the old rhyme spreads itself over a mere five openings, but each reveals such a vista of action and fun that perusal with repetition could take an hour or more. Each double spread sports five separate flaps; each flap, being opened, reveals animals in hiding places from the likely to the inconceivable. Chickens roost in a chamber pot beneath a bed, there is a cow in the clothes basket . . riotous nonsense in an appropriately colourful art style make of this a book for a child whose spirits need a boost. (For a more conventional version, see Book List 1, page 29.)

1 Hunter Pat Hutchins (Bodley Head/Puffin paperback)

More than a mere counting book, this amusing volume tells a mute story which ultimately has the hero – a determined if unobservant big game hunter – in full flight before his intended victims. This artist's work is here, as ever, colourful and vigorous. The progressive theme gives full rein to her flair for design; each double spread seems to improve with examination. Some of the inherent irony may be lost on the three-to-fours, but the action and humour will delight.

Our Cat Flossie Ruth Brown (Andersen Press)
This book describes, simply, the likes and habits of a loved family cat. The illustrations are beautiful in the extreme, and the combination evokes the nature of domestic cats in a gentle, unspectacular way. (She's unable to resist a box . . .) The clear text will certainly help the early reader; and the cover, with Flossie's yellow eyes staring boldly from her thick, tabby fur, is an added joy. This book could be acquired at three, read alone at six and loved forever, if cats are part of the child's family life.

The Outside Cat Jane Thayer, illus. Feodor Rojankovsky (Hodder & Stoughton/Knight paperback)
'Samuel was an outside cat. He was an outside cat because he never was allowed inside.' But he was also a cat of resource and determination; and luck was, in the end, on his side. The illustrations do this robust tale justice; they are clear, bright and, in places, dramatic.

Peter's Chair Ezra Jack Keats (Bodley Head)
Peter's apprehension about baby Susie's tendency to take over all his possessions reaches the limit when it comes to his little chair. Only his ultimate realization that he really is a big brother – far too big for the chair – and Dad's wise suggestion that Peter help paint it for the baby, defuse the situation. Keats is an enterprising artist. His work, a combination of collage and vivid colour, is arresting. There is a masterly matching of word and picture in this book.

The Snowy Day Ezra Jack Keats (Puffin paperback)
This is a simple and satisfying book about a small boy who wakes up one morning to find that snow covers everything he can see from his window. After breakfast he dons his snowsuit and runs outside to play. His activities are described simply and precisely; it is the illustrations, a combination of collage and

vivid colour, which give the book its true individuality. Twenty-five years old this year, *The Snowy Day* is a likely candidate for classic status. (The same engaging Peter stars in *Peter's Chair*, page 121)

Pumpkin, Pumpkin Jeanne Titherington (Julia MacRae)
Gently realistic pictures and very simple text tell the story of Jamie, and the pumpkin he grows from a seed. The growth process is seen in close-up and the small boy's involvement is carefully documented. At the end, Jamie uses his pumpkin to carve a Hallowe'en face. 'But . . . he saved six pumpkin seeds for planting in the spring.' A well-rounded, satisfying story, sensitively illustrated.

*_A Rainbow of My Own_ Don Freeman (World's Work)   Out of print at the time of writing but available from libraries.

Red is Best Kathy Stinson, illus. Robin Baird Lewis (Oxford/Oxford paperback)
Red is certainly the key colour in this eye-catching book. A bright red frame rings the cover picture, and bright red end-papers lead into a book featuring red clothes of every description, page after page. The text is simple but lively; three is an age for fussiness about clothes and footwear, and the small girl pictured has a mind of her own.

*_Sally's Secret_ Shirley Hughes (Bodley Head/Puffin paperback)
All children like making houses, and Sally is no exception. The secret little house she constructs in the bushes is an enchanting place; but only when Rose comes to share it with her is Sally really happy. The pictures tell the story in warm, bright colour and careful detail.

Scruff Gerald Rose (Bodley Head/Magnet paperback)
The front cover of this cheerful saga of doggy irresponsibility sets the tone: Scruff himself poses perkily, rose between his teeth. Scruff and Grandma go shopping. Everywhere, people clutch their noses. 'Pooh! What an awful smell!' Grandma and Scruff speculate, without conclusion. No doubt at all is entertained by Tim and Debbie when the mystified pair arrive home. 'Well I never!' said Grandma. Scruff is duly scrubbed, and rinsed and brushed . . . The pictures are hearty in Gerald Rose's best tradi-

tion, generous in both number and colour, with that humorous comment on proceedings which is always, in this artist's work, set at child level.

The Shopping Basket John Burningham (Cape/Picture Lions paperback)

On the first page red-headed, bespectacled Steven is besought by a rather frayed-looking Mum to 'Pop down to the shop . . . and buy six eggs, five bananas, four apples, three oranges for the baby, two doughnuts and a packet of crisps . . .' The mission is simply accomplished, but more than usual difficulties attach to the journey home. In turn, a bear, a monkey, a kangaroo, a goat, a pig and an elephant confront Steven and demand the eggs, the bananas . . . Cleverly, Steven contrives to part with only one of each commodity, and hurry on home – to a mother who asks 'How could it have taken so long?' The illustrations are vintage Burningham, and include diagram-style pictures of the items bought, depleted at each encounter. Good fun and counting practice.

* The Tale of the Turnip Anita Hewett, illus. Margery Gill (Bodley Head)

Thomas Builds a House

Thomas Goes Out

Thomas Goes to the Doctor all by Gunilla Wolde (Hodder & Stoughton)

Three more 'Thomas' titles, all reflecting three-year-old interests and activities. Small, sound little books, written with sensitivity and humour. (See also the 'Emma' books, companion to 'Thomas' and, in the main, suitable for this age group.)

* The Three Bears and 15 Other Stories Anne Rockwell (Hamish Hamilton)

Wake up, Bear Lynley Dodd (Spindlewood)

Bear has been asleep for many months, and the other animals think it is time for him to wake up. All encouragement fails – even a watery whoosh from elephant's trunk leaves Bear sleeping soundly. In the end, they all retreat, and a wandering bee comes buzzing past. ' "Honey!" said Bear, and he woke up.' The age-old formula is here seen at work to perfection, with

Lynley Dodd's genial animals, all drawn with style and humour, certain to capture attention.

What Do People Do All Day? Richard Scarry (Collins)

When We Were Very Young A. A. Milne (Methuen/Methuen paperback)

This is the first Christopher Robin and Pooh Bear poetry book, and should be available for all three-year-olds. You will have your favourites among the poems, and may want to defer using some until four or five. But a proportion of these verses are so three-ish that they should not be missed.

Where the Wild Things Are Maurice Sendak (Bodley Head/Puffin paperback)

About Max, who sails off 'through night and day and in and out of weeks and almost over a year to where the wild things are'. There is no better example than this, among picture books, of the power of the best words used in the best way, to enchant; or of the right illustrations to support and sustain. Sendak's monsters might be said to have started a monster fashion; but they are themselves unique. Lumbering, benign, ferocious but friendly, they accept Max's domination. Theirs is a dream-world from which he departs when home calls. Max's participation in their 'wild rumpus' (which lasts for three un-worded pages) is one of the highlights of modern picture-book art. An unforgettable book; a rare experience

Whistle for Willie Ezra Jack Keats (Bodley Head)

Peter cannot whistle when this story starts, and can, when it ends. His dog Willie is as pleased as everyone else, when his master's persistent practice is rewarded with success. Arresting colour and sure design complement an appealing story to produce an outstanding book. (The same little boy is the subject of *The Snowy Day*, p. 121 and *Peter's Chair*, p. 121.)

Wilberforce Goes on a Picnic (also *Wilberforce Goes Shopping* and *Wilberforce Goes to a Party*) Margaret Gordon (Viking Kestrel/Puffin paperback)

These are gently humorous stories about a sturdy little bear and his family. Domestic drama alternates with small adventures and predictable disasters, all depicted in cheerful colour. Bears are here to stay, it seems; Wilberforce is a welcome addition.

The Winter Bear   Ruth Craft, illus. Erik Blegvad   (Collins/Picture Lions paperback)

Three children don thick clothes and set off for a walk in a snowy landscape. Between them, they pick a winter posy, chat to a cow – and find 'a brown knitted bear' caught in the bare branches of a tree. At home, they dry him, dress him, put his arm in a sling and sit him on 'a round brown cushion, in the best arm chair'. The simple, satisfying action scarcely needs the text; and the pictures are expressive and buoyant.

When I was Four . . .

When I was Five . . .

6

When I was Four,
I was not much more

When I was Five,
I was just alive

Understandable comment, in retrospect, but hardly true. The just-turned-four-year-old is much, much 'more' than she has ever been before, and certainly 'alive' – to any and every experience!

One might describe the four-year-old as 'launched'. She has cast off her three-year-old conformity and, like as not, her good manners and winning ways. She is entering a 'biff-bang' period which will exhaust you (but not her), shock the neighbours, and reduce you to frantically consider enrolling her full time at a playschool. Things get broken this year. Confrontations are unavoidable and understandable; the four-year-old is just as sure that she can look after herself as you are certain that she still needs supervision. You are both right, to a degree. She is bursting out all over, and neither you nor she has any real way of assessing where she is at any given time.

Four-year-olds express themselves volubly, and move about their world with ease, even agility. Every day seems to bring another accomplishment, another small ambition expressed or achieved. They make their way from buttons through zipfasteners to shoe laces; from spoon, through spoon and fork to knife and fork; from talking through singing to whistling. Their progress is so swift, so natural that it may be unnoticed by those around them, except in snatches. A member of the family who goes away for a few weeks may be astonished on their return by the youngster's progress.

No one else will have noticed. In fact, the four-year-old may be scolded for slopping milk on the tablecloth as she pours herself a drink when, only a week ago, she would not have attempted this feat at all. What is more, she will now watch and listen (within reason!) while you demonstrate a new skill She half believes that it *is* a skill, and not just an adult privilege so far denied her.

Her imagination is on the move too, of course, and often runs ahead of her new understanding. Increased experience brings increased fear, and expanding self-awareness may reduce the extent to which children will demand immediate support from their nearest and dearest. This self-imposed deprivation may lead to loneliness. For the first time, children may begin to hide their feelings; deny them, even to themselves.

Four-year-olds are beginning to see things from viewpoints other than their own, although they will have no awareness of this developing capacity. They will use it unconsciously, however, to put themselves in other people's places, and this may lead to new apprehension ('If that could happen to that boy, it could happen to me!'). It is understandable that some parents feel that only 'happy' stories should be read at this time. It is reasonable to suspect that the inclusion of monsters which 'roar their terrible roars' and 'roll their terrible eyes', not to mention wolves who plot to gobble up whole families of unprotected young, will merely increase the youngster's own fear of catastrophe. Rest assured; it is clear that children harbour dark and formless fears whatever we say, do, or present to them. Adult silence on the subject can be just as disastrous as a refusal to recognize developing sexuality in adolescence.

Small children need to know that other people have fears too, that these are natural, and are common to all creatures. Human beings have always played out their fears instinctively. The earliest drama, dance and music arose from people's need to externalize their feelings about themselves and their world; to communicate and share their hopes, fears, and joys. We help small children to do this when we share stories with them, when we show them that people are not powerless, that purposeful action leads to predictable result, and that hurdles can be jumped, problems overcome.

If we look carefully enough the whole purpose of fiction – of story – can be seen to be under way at this early stage.

The number of titles available for the over-fours is bewildering. To find your way to those which should not be missed because they are classics, and yet be sure to include books of every type, can seem a daunting task. You should certainly, by now, be making regular trips to the library, usually with your child. Enlist the support of librarians, telling them when your child has enjoyed a book, and asking for further suggestions. Don't be put off if co-operation is not as forthcoming as you might hope; no human institution improves until the people for whom it is provided show that they expect it to give service. Your enthusiasm may well stimulate librarian interest, and feedback about successful titles for particular age groups will surely be appreciated. Don't hesitate to criticize the authorities if you feel that the children's section is under-supplied. One young woman I know earned the librarian's lifelong gratitude when she organized a group of parents to make representations to the council on the sorry understocking of the children's department!

You may feel that your brash, somewhat bossy four-year-old disturbs the peace of the library – and you may well be right. There was a time when librarians frowned on any interruption to the almost hallowed quiet of their surroundings, but this was before they realized that if children were obliged to act like elderly men and women in libraries, they just didn't come. The secret is to take them to libraries from birth, accepting that baby noises, and later toddlers' grabbing habits, are part of the human condition and must be accommodated by the race in general – meanwhile, your-self reducing your youngster's capacity to interfere with others by judicious and good-tempered supervision. If the worst comes to the worst, you can always pick her up, smile apologetically (but confidently) and make off. One of my daughters was obliged to give up library visiting with her first child when she felt she could not face the inevitable tantrum again. Her toddler seemed to care nothing for taking books home, but shrieked with rage because she could not take one of the quaint little stools! After a search, we managed to buy one, and library visiting began again.

Increasingly, young children want to choose their *own* books, and this poses problems. All too often 'choice' is made impetuously, because the cover design appeals. Its contents may be quite unsuitable, or at best, hit-and-miss for the child's needs. To a certain extent, this problem is never solved, except by time; but it *is* a problem, especially if only one or two titles may be borrowed at a visit. Of course you welcome the youngster's increasing independence, and want to encourage initiative. But successful book provision is important too.

There is only one way in which you can lessen the chance of your child's choosing books which defeat this purpose: by interesting him or her in the *whole* book, in a natural way, instead of merely reading the story. Always, from this stage (or earlier, if the child is a really good listener) show the cover first. Run your hand appreciatively over it, and read the title and author, underlining the words as you do so. Then open the book to reveal the endpapers. In a picture book, these are usually coloured, and often decorated – and are repeated at the end of the book. Through your example, you can train your child to look in turn at endpapers and title-page, at which point you can again underline and read the title, author and publisher. You will be surprised at the interest he will find in this procedure, and how quickly he will pick up the expressions 'author', 'illustrator', 'endpapers', 'spine', 'publisher'. One of the scheme's chief benefits is that it can be used to help choose library books. The child will see the sense in examining the book well, if this has become entrenched as a habit. At all events, it will help the process of choice in the end – and his awareness of books and their unique qualities in the meantime.

One of my grandchildren, Oliver, became fascinated with endpapers when he was about five. He soon noticed that those at the end of the book sometimes varied from those at the front: slightly, in some cases, and dramatically in others. One day he asked me, 'Why aren't the front endpapers called "startpapers"?' For freshness of vision, give me young children any day!

Along with library visits must go visits to bookshops. In fact, a research programme in England established that children who come from families where books are *owned* are the best readers of all. (I don't need a scientist to tell me such an elementary fact, but I am pleased nonetheless.) Unfortunately, many adults never enter bookshops. It does seem as if the habit must start early if it is to endure. You may feel that even more problems will present themselves in a bookshop, where the bookseller must keep his stock in attractive condition for the ultimate buyer. Here again, early visiting is the key. Children soon learn that libraries and bookshops are different – and that the most 'different' bookshop advantage is that you don't have to return the book *ever*, once bought. Modern paperback publishing has brought many excellent titles within the means of average families; you needn't fear that a good bookshop will stock only expensive books. But do make sure that your child has the pleasure of owning a beautiful hard-covered edition of a much-loved book from time to time – possibly a title from the library which has been enjoyed.

A well-produced book is a thing of beauty. Learning to love such a book for its physical qualities as well as its contents is part of the process of becoming a 'real' reader – a person whose life is enriched by the sight and feel and smell of books.

If your child doesn't have her own bookcase by four, I would urge you to provide one. Simple sets of shelves can be made from planks (cut to length by a timber dealer) supported by bricks or concrete blocks. These have the advantage of being easy to move, and reassemble or extend, as the collection grows. If the youngster's very own shelves are right next to her bed, she will quickly see the point of reaching for a book when she wakes up. If only as a means of ensuring family peace in the morning, this makes sense!

Four-year-old scope is limited only by capacity, which in turn is the product of experience, temperament and innate intelligence. The range of scope is very wide, and it is easy to draw hasty conclusions about the reasons for differences. It is not difficult to understand the varying capacities of those children at each extreme of the scale; at this early level, when the child's experience of books naturally involves the mediation of a concerned family adult, it is easy to explain the bookish child's tastes and accomplishments. Similarly, at the other extreme, it is all too simple to recognize the tragic waste of human potential which has already taken place.

What about those in between? There are differences, and they must be recognized. It should not be assumed that all children can be transformed into committed readers of imaginative fiction, any more than that they can be turned into gymnasts or carpenters at will. Children inherit wide and diverse sets of characteristics, which, interacting with environment and body chemistry, determine the sort of people they become. Two and two never make four in human development; at best, three or five.

It is essential for children's best progress to accept them as they are. Some children at four will listen endlessly, their eyes glazed, their whole being so involved in the story that the real world around them does not exist. Others will listen only if the subject is one of their favourite topics, and then only in short bursts. They may keep interrupting and, jumping about – almost as if physical involvement is *their* way, and has to be practised simultaneously if the experience is to be successful. One might almost say that for *these* children, story-sessions, in whatever form they can take them, are even more necessary than for the others. Left to themselves, they might never tap the vital source that is there, in books. And reading is *different* from gymnastics and carpentry, or any other skill. At its very least, it is a tool. (Think how much has been written about gymnastics and carpentry.) At its best, it rescues readers from dependence on their own limited experience and thought, introduces them to other people, other times and other places, helps them to see shades of meaning and to discern relationships. No child should be lightly dropped from the ranks of potential readers – and the so-called 'practical' child runs this risk. Tragically, this type-casting of children draws its greatest support from the children themselves. Adult attitudes are all too easily sensed and absorbed so that many children cast themselves, early in life, as 'physical' types who will naturally kick balls, bang nails, sew cloth, *instead of* reading.

Why not all of these things? In a world in which identification of 'isms' is assuming astonishing proportions, this particular form of stereotyping (typism?) seems to go undetected. As it is universal in application and life-denying in effect, it is time we looked at it. It is *surely* one of the great dividers, taking in both sexes and all races.

And so to the books themselves.

Four-year-olds will continue to relish old favourites, meanwhile enjoying longer and more complex stories. As their own maturity increases, they will absorb more of the undertones of some stories, using their developing sensitivity to 'see' things which once flowed over and around them. For several years, their needs will hardly change, requiring for their satisfaction stories of increasing depth and detail, but similar topic and type. The essential need for illustration will be reduced slightly, but still remain important. Only the need for 'easy reading' books will vary the scene, and the timing of this phenomenon is, usually, in the hands of the educational authorities of the country in which they live.

Fortunate children of this age group – children whose introduction to books was successfully accomplished years before, and whose progress has been smooth and satisfying – will be ready, now, for some of the classics: Babar, Little Tim, the simplest of the Grimm and Andersen fairy stories and a whole host of titles, old and new, which will stir their imagination, expand their experience of people and things, make them laugh, and make them wonder.

A handsome new anthology will be welcomed as birthday or Christmas present by the four-year-old; such a book as *Tomie de Paola's Favourite Nursery Tales*. Seventeen stories, nine fables from Aesop and four poems (two Stevenson, one Longfellow and Lear's 'The Owl and the Pussy-cat'), all illustrated in de Paola's clear-lined, almost luminous style, make together a superlative book for a family, or lucky single child. Every page is framed; each is more than generously endowed with illustrations in rich but soft colour. This big, satisfying book might well be provided a year earlier; but a proportion of the tales, as well as the fables, are more suitable for five-year-old listeners, and the book will last, once acquired.

Rather than extend this chapter to a tedious length (and because there is such a wealth of diverse and wonderful material available at this stage) I have used the Book List to provide details of many of these titles. Remember that this List and the others throughout the book constitute an essential part of the whole. Correctly used – and with reference to the instructions for obtaining books given in the Introduction – the 'Books to Use' sections should rescue you

from that 'Where do I go from here?' confusion which I remember
so well from my own early parenthood.

I have felt it practical to deal with this two-year period (roughly
covering four- to six-year-olds) in one section. The assumption is
that, although the four-to-sixes are diverse in many ways, they
have much in common, and are moving at their own pace through
the same landscape.

Without exception, they have a taste for realism. What other
people are doing, how it all works . . . four-to-sixes want to know.
It would be very boring if this garnering of fact and deepening of
insight could be accomplished only through books about people.
Fortunately, heroes and heroines can be animals, vehicles, houses
– there is no restriction.

An agreeable number of modern picture books do, however,
present the small child against a recognizable family background,
immersed in the typical concerns of everyday life. *Dogger* by Shirley
Hughes concerns the loss and subsequent restoration of a much-
loved cuddly toy called Dogger. The small hero, Dave, is independent and sturdy, inclined to seriousness, and rather overshadowed
by his older sister Bella. His family is splendid. They all see
Dogger's loss as a real tragedy, Dave's mute grief as the anguish it
is. Shirley Hughes draws children's outsides in a way which leaves
no doubt about her knowledge of their insides. Her stories are as
sure-footed as her illustrations are perceptive. In *Moving Molly*, a
small girl's loneliness after the family moves house is resolved in
the only possible way when she finally, triumphantly, makes
friends. These are not small concerns; they are universal. The
youngster who meets them in picture and print is involved in
human apprehension and its joyful resolution.

There are now four books devoted to the life and times of Katie
Morag McColl, and they are all well worth searching out. The
stories, simple in themselves, concern the trials, triumphs and everyday concerns of a small Scottish girl. Ordinary enough, you might
say; and certainly, Katie Morag's affairs are hardly sensational. It
is the setting that makes the difference, and the characters whom
this able author-artist – Mairi Hedderwick – has created and
brought to life. For Katie Morag and her family live on the Isle of

Struay off the north-west coast of Scotland, and the reader takes up residence with them in no uncertain terms, from the first page.

To begin with, there are the endpapers, identical in each of the books. In turn, they show the small island settlement in the full light of busy, clamorous day and indolent, quiet night. Both wide, landscape illustrations, in delicate watercolour, are planned in chart-like detail to reveal the small harbour, ringed with buildings and other features which the reader, with the characters, will come to know: the 'Shop and Post Office' which is Katie Morag's home, the jetty whose role is central to island affairs, the five cottages, with their varied occupants, the long road round to the five farms on the opposite shore, the last of which belongs to Katie Morag's 'Grannie Island'. The illustrations in each book adhere scrupulously to the original. The characters are easily recognized, and panoramic background views reveal earth, sea and sky in different moods but identical detail. Novelty is introduced in the age-old way of islands, by the arrival of visitors: Granma Mainland, who bodes fair to be a drawback but in the end becomes (unwittingly) an asset; the five 'big boy cousins' who create such chaos but finally settle down, aided and abetted in all their moods by their eager 'small girl cousin'. The clutter and paraphernalia of indoor and outdoor life in a vigorous working community are here in glorious plenty – as are warm hearts, strong personalities (most of them female, for good measure) and the smells and sensations of life lived close to soil and sea. (These books are available in paperback, but do lose something in the conversion. Try to own at least one hardback, for the 'map' alone.)

Parents often ask me for a book about active, assertive girls and women, and the Katie Morag stories certainly fill this bill. Fortunately, there are many more such available – though I insist that choice should be made on a wide, rather than narrow set of criteria. A book is not a good book because of its subject. It is a good book if its subject is incidental to its real strengths, which must number a plot which has pace and shape, characters who come alive, satisfactory resolution of action and (always present in the books which go on from generation to generation) a certain quality which I can only describe as virtuosity.

Some of these qualities are present in *Phoebe and the Hot Water Bottles*, by Terry Furchgott and Linda Dawson. Phoebe is a small girl whose father, an ageing chemist who cares for her alone, can never see beyond hot water bottles as birthday and Christmas presents. Phoebe ends up with a whole fleet (157!) which she tends with love, nurses in sickness, educates, and takes to the pantomime for a treat. Phoebe is real. She has strength, a finely-tuned understanding of her weary Dad's limitations, and real resource in emergency. She runs her own show, does Phoebe, and her book has style. (One of my grandchildren, when consulted about her hopes in the Christmas present stakes one December, said without faltering, 'One hundred and fifty-seven hot water bottles!')

Every now and then a book appears which seems to have an almost breathtaking number of successful ingredients. Such a book is *The Lighthouse Keeper's Lunch* by Ronda and David Armitage. Lighthouses – particularly set, as this one is, in a panorama of blue sky and smooth sea, with a line reaching to a house on the cliff down which a basket of delicious food comes each day – can hardly fail. Mrs Grinling's battle to divert the seagulls from their dastardly habit of purloining the lunch is funny in the extreme. The language has individuality, without any dreary intention to teach, and the illustrations are colourful and detailed.

The Lighthouse Keeper's Catastrophe, appearing years after the original story, is more than a mere sequel: it is a splendidly original tale in its own right. It all begins when Mr Grinling, exasperated with Hamish the cat who has just polished off the fish his master and mistress have spent the morning catching, locks both cat and, carelessly, *keys* in the lighthouse. Thereafter mishap builds on mischance to produce calamity. The ultimate solution hearkens back hilariously to the line-and-pulley burlesque of the first book. The absurdly bumbling lighthouse keeper and his resourceful never-say-die wife – not to mention the incorrigible Hamish – contrive to create astonishing chaos in an apparently idyllic situation, to the certain joy of young reader-viewers and their elders.

Ronda and David Armitage have perfected a divided-page, almost comic-strip technique to vary the traditional whole-page treatment of their picture books, and this is seen again to advantage in *Don't Forget, Matilda!*, a story about a family of koalas. Matilda is the sturdy, forceful small daughter whose father looks after her while her mother works. Father is genial and efficient, but both he and Matilda are inclined to forget things. The pages of this splendid book are crammed without being cluttered. 'Learning points' abound, again, without over-earnest intention. Family relationships are warm ('Perhaps a little something would take away the ache,' suggested Father) – but realistic ('Well, you'll just have to walk.'). Attention is guaranteed; action and humour abound. This koala family is a welcome change from badgers and bears, but certainly in the same warm and woolly tradition.

Frances is a badger, and she has already made her place in children's fiction. Set comfortably in a loving family, with kindly but not-to-be-victimized parents, she comes to terms with night-time fears (*Bedtime for Frances*), the arrival of competition (*A Baby Sister for Frances*) and several other typical apprehensions and reversals. Why badgers, or koalas – or bears – instead of humans? Why not? Frances and Matilda, in their separate small persons, embody all small girls. Perhaps their animal forms allow them to *be* all small girls in a way human form would not? Or maybe children, who like small furry animals, just enjoy identifying with them; the 'moral' is perhaps blurred at the edges, the point taken more painlessly. Minarik's *Little Bear* has this same quality in his dealings with his family. He is all children, perhaps because of, rather than despite, his furry coat and clumsy bear paws. Certainly, these books seem to teach less obviously than some with real-child characters.

There are two books about Titch, and at first sight they may seem suitable for the twos and threes. No harm will be done, certainly, by acquiring either or both at an early stage, but the consideration of size and status is a strong four-year-old preoccupation, and Titch speaks loudly to this older group. Pat Hutchins both wrote and illustrated the books and her text is brief, to the point of sparseness. What it does not say is as significant as what it does.

> Titch was little.
> His sister Mary was a bit bigger.
> And his brother Pete was a lot bigger.

> Pete had a great big bike.
> Mary had a big bike.
> And Titch had a little tricycle . . .

The illustrations, brightly coloured, are seen against a plain white background. On all but one double spread, only the children and the objects mentioned are depicted. The middle spread demonstrates this gifted artist's flair for design, with green hill, yellow buildings and darker green trees creating a perfect setting for the kites which wheel in the sky above; and for the children on either side, Pete and Mary holding tight to their kite strings, and Titch clutching his pinwheel.

Titch himself is an uncompromisingly steadfast little figure, always bringing up the rear, never complaining. He has his moment of reward and glory when the seed he plants grows, and grows and *grows*. On the last page he allows himself a smug little smirk, while older brother and sister exclaim in wonder. In the second book, *You'll Soon Grow into Them, Titch*, the small protagonist is seen first demonstrating that his own clothes are too small for him – and then establishing that cast-offs from higher up the family are certainly a bit too big. Mum and Dad agree that '. . . Titch should have some new clothes' and Dad takes him shopping. The observant viewer may just notice Mum's knitting – and her considerable girth – throughout; Titch gives his outgrown apparel to the new baby with a histrionic flourish. 'He'll soon grow into them,' said Titch. Over-four independence needs plenty of this red-blooded stuff to grow on.

In its less arrogant moments, it needs reassurance, too. Confirmation of parental love which is unconditional and total, not to be withdrawn now that babyhood is being left behind, manners are becoming brash, contours harshening. *Little Gorilla* by Ruth Bornstein speaks to any child who wonders in his innermost heart about his place in the world. It is, in a deep sense, about love and acceptance.

> Once there was a little gorilla, and everybody
>   loved him.
> His mother loved him.

> His father loved him.
> His grandma and grandpa and his aunts and
> uncles loved him.
> Even when he was only one day old, everybody
> loved Little Gorilla . . .

Inevitably, Little Gorilla grows.

> And one day, Little Gorilla was BIG!

Here, thinks the small listener, comes the crunch. But

> . . . everybody came, and everybody sang
> 'Happy Birthday Little Gorilla!'
> And everybody still loved him.

Certainly simple enough in both word and picture for two- and three-year-olds; but speaking most directly to the 'launched' over-four, making his way in the world with his heart in his mouth.

As a picture book this has true virtuosity. Little Gorilla himself avoids both the smart alecky and the sentimentalized monkey image. He is engaging but not coy, mischievous but not slick. The book itself is beautifully designed; its impact is immediate and eloquent. Against a soft green background, Little Gorilla, his family and friends come alive as characters of good humour and diverse temperament. The reaction of Giraffe, Elephant and other animals who suffer (cheerfully or resignedly) from Little Gorilla's ebullience is inferred, not stated. This is a perfect picture book.

By the same token, Pat Hutchins's *Happy Birthday, Sam* touches on a four-year-old concern: the frustration of *feeling* old enough to dress yourself, but of not being tall enough to reach your clothes hanging in the wardrobe – or the taps, when you know you can brush your own teeth . . . The neat resolution of Sam's problem is inspirational. Grandpa's present proves to be a sturdy little chair which allows Sam to service himself completely, and to sail his new boat in the sink.

> 'Its the nicest boat ever,' he said, 'and
> the nicest little chair.'

This title, also, is so triumphantly simple in both text, and bold, brisk picture, that you may mistake it for a two-year-old book. But it is a four-year-old book in all its fibres. One knows without being told that it was written by an informed and feeling parent for *her* 'turning' four-year-old.

The need for a short – or longer – stay in hospital is quite common among young children, and parents may feel that a book on the subject will help. Certainly, there are several sound little 'documentaries' on the subject. Hamish Hamilton has published a set of small, inexpensive books by Nigel Snell, and this includes *Lucy Loses her Tonsils, Ruth Goes to Hospital, Tom Visits the Dentist* and a host of other stories ranging from *Sally Moves House* to *Sam's New Dad*.

However, I have never been sure that this serious, factual preparation for the experience offers the reassurance parents are hoping to provide; and this doubt extends to other situations, from facing a new baby in the family to being adopted, starting school, or whatever experience supposedly threatens the child's security. A story which is set against the relevant background is certainly likely to provide more enjoyment than a sober statement of procedure.

One of my grandchildren spent many months of her first four years in hospital. *Crocodile Medicine*, by Marjorie-Ann Watts, a dead-pan story about a crocodile patient who disrupts hospital routine but enchants a small fellow patient, had her total, enraptured attention when I produced it for her. This title is now out of print, but a splendid successor, *Crocodile Teeth*, would have received equally joyful approval, I am confident.

Between its cheerfully colourful covers, the same crocodile, obviously now a staple feature of the ward, is seen to be in some distress, copious tears pouring over a swollen cheek. 'Toothache!' diagnoses the doctor; and Julie has the job of persuading – compelling – the great cowardly creature to submit to the kindly but firm ministrations of the dentist. Two for the price of one here! What to expect at the dentist emerges in the most explicit way as Crocodile loses a decayed tooth and has a filling. There is so much to look at, and it is all depicted with such precision, colour and clarity in the well-designed double-spread illustrations, that a child either in or out of hospital could not fail to be charmed.

And of course, blissfully, there is Madeline, whose midnight dash through the streets of Paris to the hospital has been so dramatically documented by Ludwig Bemelmans. Later, she is visited by the other eleven little girls who live with her 'in an old house in Paris that was covered in vines . . .' at which stage Madeline steals the show, as usual.

> *But the biggest surprise by far,*
> on her stomach was a scar!

Many years ago, visiting American friends gave our children their own copy of this notable book. It slipped immediately into all our hearts; and on to our tongues, too, for its compelling, exuberant verse was soon in daily use among us.

> *And afraid of a disaster,*
> *Miss Clavel ran fast and faster!*

The book itself seemed quite wonderfully, extravagantly, large to our children, accustomed as they were to post-war New Zealand austerity. And the exotic fly-away pictures were savoured as wonders from another world, as indeed they were. I have never forgotten the family's return from a regular Friday-night library visit a few years later. All of them seemed to fall through the door at once, shouting – from the twelve-year-old down – 'Mum! – *There's another Madeline*!' Their father reported that the fuss in the library had drawn disapproving looks from unencumbered adults selecting their weekend reading, but that Miss Fisher – *our* librarian, always on the side of the kids – had beamed. The new book was *Madeline's Rescue*, and there she was again, reckless, intrepid child, risking life and limb *and* Miss Clavel's sanity in the very shadow of the Eiffel Tower and the bridges over the Seine. (A priceless bonus, this artist's genius for bringing the sights and sounds of London and Paris alive.) Between 1952 and 1962, five more Madeline books were published in London. They are all currently in print, and should not be missed. As an antidote to over-seriousness and the dull realism with which all too many modern adults would beleaguer children, *Madeline* is un-alloyed treasure. The wonderful doggerel verses, outrageously flouting all rules of scansion, grammar and good taste, lodge in the mind:

> *Poor Miss Clavel, how would she feel*
> *If she knew that on top of the Ferris wheel,*
> *In weather that turned from bad to rotten,*
> *Pepito and Madeline had been forgotten?*
>
> *As a diet there is nothing worse*
> *Than green apples and roses for an old horse.*
> *'Dear lady' said Miss Clavel 'we beg your pardon.*
> *It seems our horse has eaten up your garden.'*

and

> *It serves you right you horrid brat*
> *For what you did to that poor cat!*

Incomparable stuff for the deserving young.

To return to the subject of books which may help children to face difficult or frightening situations: *The Tenth Good Thing About Barney*. Erik Blegvad's sensitive, black-and-white picture shows a small boy sitting at a table, forehead on fist.

> *My cat Barney died last Friday.*
> *I was very sad.*
>
> *I cried, and I didn't watch television.*
> *I cried, and I didn't eat my chicken or even*
> *the chocolate pudding.*
> *I went to bed, and I cried.*

His mother suggests that he '. . . should think of ten good things about Barney', so that he could 'tell them at the funeral' – so he does.

> *I thought, and I thought, and I thought of good*
> *things about Barney.*
> *I thought of nine good things. Then I fell asleep*

Later, he helps his father in the garden, and learns about the earth, and its relationship with living things.

> 'Things change in the ground,' said my father.
> 'In the ground everything changes.'
>
> 'Will Barney change too?' I asked him.

'Oh yes,' said my father.
'He'll change until he's part of the ground in the
     garden.'

'And then,' I asked, 'will he help to make flowers
     and leaves?'

'He will,' said my father.
'He'll help to grow the flowers, and he'll help to
     grow that tree and some grass.'

Here is consolation of the best kind.

For the oldest children in the group under discussion *Badger's
Parting Gifts*, by Susan Varley, offers a version of death in old age,
its acceptance by those bereaved, and an assurance of the nor-
mality of their grief. The setting of this sensitive yet down-to-earth
story has a *Wind in the Willows* flavour; the animals, Mole, Frog,
Fox and Rabbit live as neighbours in a woodland setting, all
of them profiting from old Badger's kindness and wisdom. When
he dies – which he does willingly – they are initially devastated.
'All the animals had loved Badger, and everyone was very sad.
Mole especially felt lost, alone and desperately unhappy.'

Winter intervenes and the animals must cope with their sorrow
as the snow covers their homes. With the approach of spring,
visiting begins again, and they find themselves increasingly talking
about Badger and the way he had helped all of them to learn
individual skills. 'He had given them each a parting gift to treasure
always. Using these gifts they would be able to help each other.'

The illustrations in this original book have a quality which is
haunting; there is at once cosy domestic warmth and the beauty
and harshness of nature, the inevitability of the seasons somehow
echoing and reinforcing the certainties of birth, life and death.

I'll Always Love You, by Hans Wilhelm, is ostensibly about the
death of a pet; but it is also about life, and how it can be lived
richly. A boy tells us about 'Elfie – the best dog in the whole
world', of how he and she grew up together . . . 'but Elfie grew
much faster than I did' . . . and of how Elfie died when he was still
a boy and she was an old dog. We see his love for Elfie in action;
they are just as boisterous as one expects boy and dog to be, and

the boy tells the dog every night 'I'll always love you,' and believes that she understands. There is humour, as well as pathos in the picture of the youngster toiling upstairs bearing the elderly Elfie; and the family grief, as they bury the loved old dog together, is expressive, but not sentimental. The boy's good sense is revealed as he refuses a new puppy. 'Someday I'll have another dog, or a kitten, or a goldfish. But whatever it is, I'll tell it every night: "I'll always love you."' This simple story demonstrates, superbly, the capacity of a good piece of fiction to suggest to readers of any age, useful ways of coping with unavoidable loss, and of enjoying those we love, be they people or animals.

It's no use asking me for a book to help a child face, or come to terms with, the death of a parent. I can only suggest that all books which are good, honest, loving books have a capacity to help people understand that life is shadow as well as light, sorrow as well as laughter, and that we all have to come to terms with it in our own way. Human scars heal in the end in a climate of love, goodwill and good humour. Don't waste time looking for a particular book in an emergency; the best book will be the one that diverts, amuses, engrosses, stirs the imagination and warms the heart. Such a book may well create a climate in which emotion can be expressed, and this is infinitely more important than 'understanding'. How can anyone, adult or child, 'understand' the death of another loved person?

However, there are many occasions in a child's life when a book may help him to accept or adjust to a particular situation. It is understandable that parents should be eager to find and use these books as need arises, but essential that they should be good books in their own right; not merely a book about new babies, going to playschool, the doctor, the dentist, the barber or whatever. *A Brother for Momoko* was so exactly right for my eldest grandchild when she stayed with me at three-and-a-half while her baby brother was born, that the experience of reading it to her was breathtaking. One felt Nicola experiencing that book with her eyes, her ears, her whole body. It was somehow, instantly, part of her. Such an experience must remain with a child always, however 'forgotten' the book. Iwasaki's sensed-rather-than-seen knowledge of, and feeling for, a tiny girl who just turned into a big sister is delicately but strongly transmitted, both by word and illustration, in this superb book.

> He is tiny and soft and warm.
> And he is my very own brother.

Regrettably, *A Brother for Momoko* is out of print as I write. I do not want to believe that it is gone forever, and so have left it intact rather than allow it to become a casualty of this revision. (You will note that I have done this with some other dearly loved titles.) The library may be able to help, meanwhile.

Like most institutions in our society, adoption is changing in form. There is a growing tendency for adoptive parents to stay in touch with the child's natural mother – or father, under some circumstances. If this practice ever becomes universal, the need for a special book on adoption may evaporate. After all, it's *not knowing* where you come from, and why your original parents were unable to bring you up, that is potentially upsetting. I suspect that the rapidly changing scene in this field is responsible for the lack of books with an adoption theme at the moment. Significantly, there are novels for teenagers available on this subject, probably reflecting the harsher official attitudes of earlier years, with ensuing problems. Most of these deal with an adolescent's search for a parent; a theme which will virtually disappear if openness on all fronts becomes the norm. Perhaps, some day, we will have picture books in which young children are confronted by the problems inherent in having adoptive parents for every day, and one or more natural parents for visiting. After all, twenty years ago it would have been unthinkable to publish a book for very young children in which a small boy goes home to his mother after an outing with his father, who is clearly living apart from them; and yet we have *Are We Nearly There?* today (see p. 112).

Solo parents are commonplace in picture books these days; Phoebe and her elderly Dad have their counterpart in Alex and his youngish Mum about whom Mary Dickinson has written five books. These are brisk, cheerful stories with an urban setting which is graphically portrayed in bold colour by Charlotte Firmin. Relationships are democratic. Alex and his Mum bicker and laugh together, and come out on top. Mum must certainly be acceptable to the feminists among us; she builds Alex a bed on stilts when he runs out of floor space in his tiny room. *Alex's Bed* is the first story. The other titles are listed at the end of this chapter.

Children who are mentally handicapped often receive very cruel treatment from normal children. This is usually generated by feelings of curiosity and self-consciousness in the face of 'odd' behaviour or looks; even by fear. Some sort of preparation is desirable, and, as ever, a book always helps. *Don't Forget Tom* is an excellent 'documentary' about a mentally handicapped child. Tom lives in a loving and caring family. His sister and brother are normal, and, with their parents' wise assistance, try to help Tom to have fun, to learn, to cope with his problems. The excellent coloured photographs depict a family of real people getting on with their separate lives and accommodating a handicapped member with courage and honesty. This is not a book for 'different' children but for their sisters, brothers and all other children. And adults too; we have a long way to go before the handicapped children of the world receive their share, as of right.

In like category is *Ben*, by Victoria Shennan, a small book in the same series as *I Am Adopted*. Here, a boy with Down's Syndrome is depicted as a youngster who, with the help of family and friends, can enjoy normal activities. Good sense and warm feelings emerge from Ben. I would like to think that parents of well-equipped (so-called 'normal') children make the necessary moves to ensure that the children become familiar with the plight of less fortunate youngsters. Such a book will help.

It is natural that parents will want their children to learn about life in other countries; and disappointing, when documentary-type books do not hold their interest. What is needed is a steady supply of picture books which succeed in involving the child through the force of their story, their creation of characters who come alive, the relevance of theme to children's lives everywhere. Such a book is *Not So Fast, Songololo*, and I venture to suggest that any child who comes to know and love this book will have little trouble identifying with black South Africans, regardless of the politics of their elders.

Shepherd is any small child, anywhere, pleased to be accompanying his Granny to town because, as his Mama says, 'He is a big boy now.' Gogo, his grandmother is old '. . . but her face shines like new school shoes. Her hands are large and used to hard work, but when they touch, they are gentle.' Gogo understands the ways and dreams of small boys, and knows that Shepherd's sneakers (his 'tackies') are old and secondhand. Somehow, money that might have provided Gogo with new shoes (hers are like '. . . worn-out tyres on an old car') is used instead to buy Shepherd a pair of new red-and-white tackies. 'Shepherd feels so happy that it hurts him just to sit still.'

Nothing is said in this well-favoured book about Gogo's tiredness throughout the long journey by bus and on foot, though Niki Daly's picture of the old woman dozing, hands in lap, in the bus terminus while 'Songololo' (his grandmother's pet name for him) sits, knees under chin, gloating over his new shoes, conveys a wealth of fact, as well as feeling. There is a radiance about *Not So Fast, Songololo* which will be felt by all who experience it, young or old.

Facts about human reproduction can be taught very easily at this stage, and most parents will be helped along this particular path by the provision of suitable books. What is suitable? How much information does a child need by the time he begins school, for example? Physical differences pose no particular problems in families or groups where there are children of both sexes, and where parents and other adults are natural and unselfconscious about bodily functions. My own experience leads me to believe that children who have not been made to feel uneasy about the topic will ask questions when they start to wonder. Certainly, the knowledge that babies grow inside their mothers should be given at first opportunity. Even if they have stopped producing children themselves, most parents can turn a pregnant friend or relation to good use here.

A strong case can be made for giving information about sexual intercourse long before the topic has any emotional significance for the child. The details will be received calmly and naturally at this early stage, and will certainly lessen the chance of later shock. But be warned: it is not uncommon for a young child to forget the whole thing, and ask again later. (It is easy to understand adult exasperation with this phenomenon!) Try to avoid books which sentimentalize birth or the facts of sex (this was very common in the literature of the forties and fifties). Nothing convinces a child more quickly that there is something unpleasant about a subject than the adoption of a 'sweetness and light' tone on the part of the adults in his life.

This is one area where you must have your heart in your policy. There are good books available, and I have listed some of them in the next Book List. I recommend that you read any book carefully before using it. There is such a wide range of reaction (among adults, I suspect, rather than children) to this emotion-charged topic that you must come to terms with your own views and decide upon a course of action or delay. Fumbling over the text of a book you have not read is not to be risked! (Take heart: your five-year-old is likely to think human functioning matters less than the way Dad's new motor-mower works – or become so bored that you decide jointly to move on to *Mike Mulligan and his Steam Shovel*.)

Now is the time to introduce the occasional story without pictures. In fact, I feel that the fourth birthday might well be marked by the acquisition of one of the collections mentioned below, or in the Book List. Have you ever told a child a story which you invented as you went along – and felt her close attention to the words, almost *seen* the picture she was building up in her mind? This is what happens – what *must* happen – when, later, children read to themselves. They must carry the image in their minds, modifying it, building on it, taking the action a step further . . . What better time to start giving practice than now?

To Read and to Tell is one of my favourite books for this purpose. My own well-worn copy bears testimony to the use it has had over the years. In this anthology Norah Montgomerie has collected a wide range of stories, conveniently grouped under headings: 'First Tales to Tell', 'Stuff and Nonsense', 'Animal Fables', 'Stories Round the Year', 'Heroes and Heroines' and 'Once Upon a Time'. Each of the ninety-eight stories might make a picture book, if illustrated; the tales vary somewhat in length and complexity but many are suitable for good listeners of just over four. Try using one of the shortest stories first, perhaps from 'First Tales to Tell'. Sandwich your performance between two picture books, if you anticipate opposition to the 'no-picture' nature of your chosen story. Say, perhaps: 'Let's have a story from this book. See if you can make the pictures in your head.'

Don't miss the opportunity to point out the 'Contents' list in the front of the book, briefly telling the youngster about the different sections. She may like to choose the section to be tapped first; in this case, accede to her request, merely choosing one of the shorter stories from the section. It will help, obviously, if you have made yourself familiar with the stories beforehand. You may be surprised at the interest she shows in the 'Contents' pages, and the expertise she develops in finding 'her' stories at subsequent encounters. This identification is the beginning of the reading process. As you read a possible title, always run your finger under the words at the speed you are speaking.

Sara and Stephen Corrin are names which you will encounter from this point on; their excellent series of collected stories for various age groups will provide a rich source through the whole of childhood, for the fortunate youngster. *Stories for Under-Fives* is the place to start – and a lively place it is. Twenty-six stories range from the fanciful to the down-to-earth, and include a valuable sprinkling of tales which were once available in picture-book form. Others, such as 'Teddy Robinson and the Band' and 'My Naughty Little Sister at the Party', give tantalizing snippets from longer collections devoted to the escapades of these notable characters, and a dash of traditional material leavens the whole. This book, and its successors, are all available in paperback versions and could be collected, with profit, as the years roll by. The hard-covered editions are so well produced, however, that I would favour acquiring at least one or two, for lasting use. (All children *must* have at least a few beloved books to hand on to *their* children – and paperbacks just will not stay the course.) Black-and-white line pictures by Shirley Hughes grace each volume, and the covers are particularly attractive.

There are many fairly simple, well-written collections of stories for the four- and five-year-olds, and I have covered the field more fully in my next book, *Five to Eight*. I hope that you will use it; meanwhile, a few more suggestions could keep you going.

Eileen Colwell's collections, *Tell Me a Story*, *Tell Me Another Story* and *Time for a Story* between them provide a wealth of usable tales, and are fortunately available in inexpensive paperback editions. One in the car, one in the kitchen and one in the bedroom would solve a lot of problems!

When I was writing *Five to Eight*, I was irked to discover that a book which had been recently tested and proven with young grandchildren – *The New Red Bike and Other Stories* by Simon Watson – was out of print. In the interim it has reappeared, divided into two parts, in the Young Puffin imprint. (The first keeps the original title and the second is called *The Picture Prize*.) These are engrossing stories of everyday family life; short and full of fun.

A modern confusion over the role of Christianity in children's lives needs facing, and resolving. Parents who are not themselves religious, and wish their children to come to their own conclusions as they grow up, are often reluctant to introduce any stories which have Christian associations. It is a great shame if this reluctance deprives children of seven years and over of the rousing (often bloodthirsty) Old Testament tales. In the early years, it is the story of the Nativity which is most likely to be omitted from listening experience.

Christmas is an important festival in all children's lives, regardless of its implications; and the Nativity story is one of the most simple and yet awe-inspiring ever told. There is something universally satisfying in the thought of a child who was destined for lasting glory beginning his life in a humble barn, the child of humble parents. Regard it as a legend, a folk-myth if you will, but don't spurn it any more than you would any other legend, because you fear indoctrination.

I would go further, and make certain that all young children grew to know and love the most beautiful version of all, that from the Gospel of St Luke:

> And she brought forth her firstborn son, and
> wrapped him in swaddling clothes, and laid
> him in a manger; because there was no room
> for them in the inn . . .

Why should modern children be shielded from exposure to these pure, easily absorbed, time-worn phrases?

> But Mary kept all these things, and pondered
> them in her heart.

Reducing language to the flat, graded-vocabulary utterances of many modern retellings certainly makes sure that children will not ponder these things in *their* hearts! Why this deprivation, when such a splendid heritage has been forged for them by earlier generations?

Two major requirements of Nativity retellings are dignity and simplicity. Fortunately, there are several versions which fulfil these conditions, and provide infinitely more, while avoiding mention of the divine element in the story. Astrid Lindgren's *Christmas in the Stable*, with Harald Wiberg's moving, luminous illustrations, permits of any, or no interpretation. The child's parents, and the shepherds, wear modern clothing; and the kings do not appear at all. And yet the book has a pervading peace and wonder about it that is irresistible. It was produced in time for my youngest children's pleasure and is still well loved in our family.

Long Ago in Bethlehem by Masahiro Kasuya fills the same role, but is traditional in setting and character. The hazy, softly coloured illustrations are very beautiful, and the text is sure-footed.

> 'Not much of a place for a king,' a shepherd said
> softly.
> But Joseph smiled and Jesus slept and Mary was
> content.

But for total, uncompromising involvement in the glory (angels and all), the earthiness, the fear, the incomparable detail (what other baby ever received incense, myrrh, and gold?), Felix Hoffmann's version has no peer. This *Story of Christmas* begins with the Angel Gabriel announcing, and ends with Herod raging, and the holy family escaping. Every step of the story is made memorable by the formal and yet infinitely personal pictures. The baby himself is a Botticelli cherub; his parents dazed by their special role but resolute in their acceptance of it. This, for me, is the best Christmas book ever produced.

As I revise *Babies Need Books*, Hoffman's incomparable 'Christmas' book is out of print. Its inclusion in this chapter is rendered even more important by this fact. In the Preface to this edition I quoted Geoffrey Trease's wise words on the subject of out-of-print books, and I refer you to them again. If ever a picture book has 'the stuff of immortality' in it, this one has. I expect it to return.

And this is the time for poetry: No need, now, to confine yourself to nursery rhymes, with infusions of simple jingle and traditional rhyming story. All these will continue to have a place – but every manner of verse may now be tried. My own collection, *I Will Build You a House* (sequel to *For Me, Me, Me*, described in Chapter 5), is a good jumping-off point for over-fives, containing as it does a wide range of different types of poetry. Inevitably, you will use some poems more often than others, prompted by their reception. But do vary the fare. Because the child responds so quickly and spontaneously to humorous verse, you may be tempted to favour the funny examples over the more serious, and this would be a shame. Such lines as the following, from 'The Night Will Never Stay' by Eleanor Farjeon, will start to show a child how simple words can be combined in a way which makes them special. Children will not know that their senses are being prodded and their imaginations activated, but they will know that the experience is enjoyable.

> The night will never stay,
> The night will still go by,
> Though with a million stars
> You pin it to the sky;
> Though you bind it with the blowing wind
> And buckle it with the moon,
> The night will slip away,
> Like sorrow or a tune.

All children wonder about the mystery of night: its inevitability, its beauty, its secrecy. Known words which spring to mind, unspoken, in the face of this mystery not only give pleasure but form to the enigma. Security has more than one source in childhood. Access to language which defines and satisfies can be part of it.

The ordinary events and features of the natural world have fortunately received inspired attention from some of the best poets for children, and on these subjects, their work cannot date. 'April Rain Song' by Langston Hughes will spring to mind – and perhaps tongue – at bedtime:

> *The rain plays a little sleep song on our roof at night –*
> *And I love the rain*

and be complemented during a rainy day by Marchette Chute's cheerful and contrasting 'Spring Rain':

> *My hair is wet my feet are wet,*
> *I couldn't be much wetter.*
> *I fell into a river once*
> *But this is even better.*

Rainbows are as magical to children today as they must have been a million years ago. Walter de la Mare caught this wonder in his lines from 'Rainbow':

> *I saw the lovely arch*
> *Of Rainbow span the sky.*
> *The gold sun burning*
> *As the rain swept by.*

The marvel and awe of a child's first encounter with the combined wonders of rainbow, sun and rain may well remain with him or her for life, if words and experience have fused.

And please do not take too seriously my warning about the blandishments of funny verse. Easiest of all to learn, it will lighten day or night, for any age. Families will have their favourites. Understandably perhaps, Spike Milligan's 'Granny' –

> *Through every nook and every cranny*
> *The wind blew in on poor old Granny . . .*

– has a firm place in my own family. Its last verse lends itself to a crescendo build-up:

> It blew on man; it blew on beast.
> It blew on nun; it blew on priest.
> It blew the wig off Auntie Fanny –
> But most of all it blew on Granny!

And why should Ian Serraillier's racy, little-known gem go unused among the world's young?

> Aunt was on the garden seat
> Enjoying a wee nap and
> Along came a fox! teeth
> Closed with a snap and
> He's running to the woods with her
> A-dangle and a-flap and –
> Run, uncle, run
> And see what has happened.

(which becomes 'hap – *and*'!) in the best renditions.

It is in the nature of children's poetry to be repeated and re-peated, and this is a good argument for owning at least one 'big' anthology. Children take great pleasure in knowing poems by heart, and learn them easily if they hear them often. Poetry is a natural extension of nursery rhyme. Lilt and rhythm are instinctive to childhood and can be enhanced, given form and expression, by familiarity with a wide range of poetry.

> What shall I call
>   My dear little dormouse?
> His eyes are small,
>   But his tail is e-nor-mouse.
> ('The Christening' by A. A. Milne)

> I found him lying near the tree; I folded
>   up his wings.
> Oh, little bird, you never heard
> The song the summer sings.
> ('For a Bird' by Myra Cohn Livingston)

> *Spin a coin, spin a coin,*
> *All fall down;*
> *Queen Nefertiti*
> *Stalks through the town . . .*
>   (Author unknown)

Wonder enters and stays with such poetry stored in the memory.

One of my children (the first Anthony) was fascinated when he was four by Robert Louis Stevenson's poem 'Where Go the Boats?' (Even the title stirs the spirit!)

> *Dark brown is the river,*
> *Golden is the sand,*
> *It flows along forever,*
> *With trees on either hand*
>   *
> *Green leaves a-floating,*
> *Castles of the foam,*
> *Boats of mine a-boating –*
> *Where will all come home?*

This poem was Anthony's favourite; he was obviously carried away on the tide of the image it evoked for him.

> *Away down the river,*
> *A hundred miles or more,*
> *Other little children*
> *Shall bring my boats ashore.*

Hardly surprising that sailing later became one of this child's passions.

Don't neglect to point out to your child how different on the page different poems *look*. A familiar poem leaps at you from the page like an old friend. Long before he can read, your youngster will recognize the *shape* of a poem he loves, even in an unillustrated collection.

> *John had*
> *Great Big*
> *Waterproof*
> *Boots on;*

> *John had a*
> *Great Big*
> *Waterproof*
> *Hat;*
> *John had a*
> *Great Big*
> *Waterproof*
> *Mackintosh –*
> *And that*
> *(Said John)*
> *Is*
> *That.*

A. A. Milne's poem 'Happiness', from *When We Were Very Young*, with its sturdy, stomping rhythm, sounds good, even without the book. But with the book – and an adult who will point to the words as they are said – the whole thing becomes a visual experience, as well as a listening treat.

Familiarity breeds affection in this field. Years ago in an old, much-loved volume, we had a copy of Rachel Field's 'General Store'.

> *Some day I'm going to have a store*
> *With a tinkly bell hung over the door,*
> *With real glass cases and counters wide*
> *And drawers all spilly with things inside . . .*

Somehow, we contrived to lose this anthology. When one of the family mentioned the poem later, I said, 'Between us, we *must* know it by heart,' and we found that we did. But it was not the same. We needed to *see* it, its solid, all-of-a-piece bulk sitting on the left side of the detailed, black-and-white line picture.

> *It will be my store and I will say:*
> *What can I do for you today?*

Met again, in a new collection several years later, it was greeted with cries of joyful recognition. Here was an old friend; but a slightly changed, because displaced, friend. The old, lost copy was never supplanted in our hearts.

It is advisable to read poetry alone, rehearsing its rhythms and absorbing its sense, before offering it to the young. There is nothing more enjoyable than reading aloud material which you know and love yourself, and this is particularly true of poetry. The child's enjoyment will reflect yours (a well-known phenomenon in any sphere); and enjoyment that is mutual is the most intense enjoyment of all.

The Young Puffin Book of Verse should be in every child's home, with another copy in the family car for emergencies. This paperback collection contains an astonishing number of the best poems every written for children of four to eight – including 'Some day I'm going to have a store . . .' On no account face life without it!

And on the family shelves, ready for instant and constant use, I can suggest nothing better than Louis Untermeyer's *Golden Treasury of Poetry*. This big, handsome book will serve any family of children faithfully and long. Its range is truly wide, and its aspect so friendly and well designed that even a small child will browse through it happily. Joan Walsh Anglund has found, here, the opportunity to produce illustrations of variety and imagination, and she has succeeded, triumphantly. Acquiring such a collection, so that you can use appropriate poems as the children grow into them, has a lot to commend it, and will also allow you to experiment. You may well be surprised at what your child has grown into while your back has been turned!

Another comprehensive anthology (572 poems, the catalogue tells us) has appeared since this book was first published: *The Walker Book of Poetry for Children*. This almost dazing collection has the supreme advantage of Arnold Lobel's illustrations, in full colour and line drawings. The selection of poems, by Jack Prelutsky, is sure-footed. The older Golden Treasury or the newer Walker anthology? The choice must be yours; they are both outstanding.

Edward Lear is a name you will come to know if you prove to enjoy reading poetry to your children (and you will, once you start). Writing in the second half of the last century, Lear produced 'nonsense' verse which has never been surpassed. You may have tried 'A was once an Apple Pie' (Chapter 3) and *The Owl and the*

Pussy-cat (Book List 1) already. Now it is time for more. Over-fours with their robust sense of fun and almost physical enjoyment of lilt and rhyme will love the simultaneous sobriety and absurdity of Lear's work.

You may well feel, if you are meeting Lear for the first time, that his poetry is too difficult for this age group. Many children, certainly, will not be ready for it until closer to six than four – but do try 'The Jumblies' at least. This story-poem combines the advantages of a straightforward (however ridiculous) plot with vigorous yet simple language. For good measure, it has a catchy inter-verse chorus:

> Far and few, far and few,
> Are the lands where the Jumblies live;
> Their heads are green, and their hands are blue,
> And they went to sea in a Sieve.

The Jumblies – as well as *The Pobble who has no Toes* and *The Quangle Wangle's Hat* – each occur in single book form in the Grafton 'Little Books of Nonsense' set which also includes *The Owl and the Pussy-cat* which you may have tried already (see Book List 1, page 34). And Helen Oxenbury's magnificent *Quangle Wangle's Hat* brings one of the best and most spectacular of Lear's poem-extravaganzas to wonderful, bursting life in full-sized picture-book form. This is probably, with *The Owl and the Pussy-cat*, the best Lear of all.

> On top of the Crumpetty Tree
> The Quangle Wangle sat,
> But his face you could not see,
> On account of his Beaver Hat.
> For his Hat was a hundred and two feet wide,
> With ribbons and bibbons on every side
> And bells, and buttons, and loops, and lace,
> So that nobody ever could see the face
> Of the Quangle Wangle Quee.

The illustrations are magnificent; in conception, in colour, in impact.

If your enthusiasm for Lear really burgeons, you would do well to order (perhaps first from the library) a copy of *The Complete Nonsense of Edward Lear*, published by Faber and Faber. This satisfying volume has the poet's own black-and-white illustrations, which will certainly grow on you, reflecting as they do the unique qualities of Lear's farcical, ludicrous but somehow sublimely logical prose.

I have spent what may seem to be a disproportionate time on poetry at the expense of stories and non-fiction for this age group. This is because I feel strongly about the child's need to experience language which is vital, resourceful, exhilarating and harmonious, language which provides the human ear with a pointed and precise pleasure which is not available from any other source, language which is crucial to the development of intelligence and self-expression.

Our society is becoming increasingly dependent on the visual image. Television selects what we will look at; advertisements are designed so that non-readers will still get the point. Sound is often loud, strident and undifferentiated. The precise, searching, illuminating impact of good and true words is in danger of being lost against the blaring and glaring background of the modern child's world. Parents are not to blame for this, and many of them, through no fault of their own, have no real 'feeling' for the sort of language which will help their children to develop into sensitive, confident, articulate women and men. I believe that the best books, from birth, will do as much for parents as for children in this area, and at the same time keep them in touch with one another. And this is the most important thing of all.

I can hear readers asking all sorts of questions: What about sexism in children's books? Shouldn't we reject all books which show girls pursuing traditional girls' roles, boys doing all the exciting, extending things? Thousands of successful parents through the ages have taken no such drastic precautions, and have, none the less, raised vigorous, independent and self-accepting daughters – and sons. If books are good books, they engender true thought and feeling and so allow children to think clearly, to feel deeply. These children will make necessary changes in their own lives and, ultimately, in the wider world. Of course we should reject those books which subtly and insidiously convey stereotyped attitudes; but these books are likely to be poor books in any case.

The best books reflect the best thought of their times. I believe that the best modern books will help us to raise children whose minds are free from unworthy prejudice, children who can love, and laugh, and get on with the business of living. I believe also that the best modern authors are conscious of the need to avoid stereotyping; that the campaigns which concerned people have conducted over the last few decades have borne fruit, and that we have, already, a growing body of good books which reflect their influence.

During the years that have elapsed since this book was first published, considerable progress has been made in the world towards a more liberal way of looking at certain crucial issues: women's rights, the evils of racism, the desperate need for international cooperation in the interests of sheer survival. But accomplishment lags far behind expressed attitude and intention, and little seems to change. Our children are born into a world in which violence, drug abuse, prejudice and inequality are rampant. The hopes of the last century's reformers that education would banish social evils have not been realized.

What recourse does the 'ordinary' parent have, in the face of these conditions? I believe that there is a way. We increase our own satisfaction, our own sense of worth, if we find ways of fortifying our children; equipping them to face a life which, despite its evident perils, still offers the age-old satisfactions of work to be done, things to laugh at, people to love and causes to fight for.

Children are the world's only true resource. Certainly, if we cease to produce children, the world as we know it will cease to exist. Real change must be made in the lives of children, if it is to endure, for the world's hope lies with the next generation. This is an area in which parents need not feel ineffective. In fact, parents have enormous power.

This may sound sweeping and idealistic, but, like most truths, is actually simple. 'The hand that rocks the cradle' indeed 'rules the world' – though the owner of that hand should not be exclusively female, must not be constantly overtired, undervalued, deprived of companionship and support. Parents must be helped to see that their job is the most important of all, in every society; for it is.

What has this to do with books? A great deal. Through the agency of good books, lovingly shared, children can be immeasurably strengthened to face their lives. Every little bit helps, in this field, and books are not 'little bits'. A good book is huge in its implication, vast in its potential, limitless in its capacity to inspire, nourish and sustain.

Five, rising six, is a good age: calmer and more assured than the year before, with less need for aggressive assertion, greater capacity for realistic self-assessment. The here-and-now satisfies this age group. Its members, attempting in the main only what is possible, are inclined to achieve, in a steady if unspectacular way. Troublesome times may lie ahead as horizons, beyond six, roll back and back. For the time being, the world is controllable because confined; success is achievable, problems surmountable.

Fortunate nearly six-year-olds use language which is rich and resourceful to explain themselves to others, to meet their own needs, and to investigate their environments. Their imagination is active, their sense of humour at the ready for laughter, their sympathy available, their love overflowing. Language, laughter and love is the prescription; and each of these will have been fed, constantly and surely, by their contact with books, and with adults who have cared for them and have been prepared to use all the means at their disposal to help them to see the world squarely, and to use its resources wisely. With conviction, and with good reason, the six-year-old announces:

> *But now I am Six I'm as clever as clever.*
> *So I think I'll be Six now for ever and ever.*

Book List 5
Books to Use between Four and Six

The range of books available for this age group is very wide indeed, and care is necessary in selection.

I have personally used all the books listed with young children, and found them successful. (You can tell, from my comments, which ones brought down the house!)

This list is best used in conjunction with the first list in my book *Five to Eight*, which was published after the first edition of *Babies Need Books* appeared. In this present list I have concentrated on picture books; *Five to Eight* emphasizes books with less illustration and more text. A healthy mixture of both types and all possible categories is the recipe for success from now on. I have done my best to include a wide range: traditional tales, everyday stories, poetry, funny stories, books for special situations, and many more.

I hope you will enjoy them all, and keep a weather eye out for books of your own choice as well, to use with this burgeoning age group.

Airport
Building a House   both by Byron Barton   (Julia MacRae/Picture Lions paperback)

The outstanding quality of these books is clarity. The text is minimal, but there is surprising detail in the vividly coloured pictures. Whether used to reinforce experience or to impart information on unfamiliar topics, these should prove to be highly successful books, likely to be perused again and again. Younger children would certainly be attracted by both books' colour and detail, but fact-hungry four-year-olds will love them.

Alex's Bed
Alex and Roy
Alex and the Baby
Alex's Outing
New Clothes for Alex   all by Mary Dickinson, illus. Charlotte Firmin   (Deutsch/several Hippo paperback)
Alfie Gives a Hand   Shirley Hughes   (Bodley Head/Picture Lions paperback)

Alfie is invited to his nursery-school friend Bernard's birthday party, and finds the prospect both attractive and daunting. In fact, he cannot be persuaded to leave his 'old bit of blanket' at home – and once there, finds the antics of the boisterous, over-excited Bernard a little hard to take. One little girl, Min, is even more intimidated by their small host's obstreperous behaviour – until Alfie makes 'a brave decision' and stuffs his blanket under the table so that he can take Min's hand, in the Bernard-dominated games. Thereafter a grand time is had by all, and Alfie realizes that he *can* manage without his blanket, after all. Bernard's kind but exasperated Mum, Bernard himself and the other children ring so true that adult and child identify absolutely. As ever, Shirley Hughes depicts live people interacting, words and pictures splendidly in tune. (See earlier lists for other 'Alfie' titles.)

Alpaca   Rosemary Billam, illus. Vanessa Julian-Ottie   (Collins/ Picture Lions paperback)

This is the story of a well-loved and worn toy rabbit who is passed over for a new pink doll and a stuffed owl at Ellen's sixth birthday party. Alpaca's hurt is great, but fortunately the desertion is temporary. When Ellen's friend Mary offers to swap him for one of her toys, 'Ellen didn't need time to think ... "I wouldn't swap Alpaca for anything. He's always been my best friend. I can make him better."' And together the two little girls do just that, using Ellen's nursing kit. The illustrations are wonderful in their fascinating, detailed coverage of the action. They have an exuberant warmth which appeals immediately. Alpaca himself is utterly engaging. A sequel, *Alpaca in the Park*, sees him lost and found – and keeps up the standard.

Angelo   Quentin Blake   (Cape/Puffin paperback)

Angelo belongs to a long-ago family of wandering players; a happy family who enjoy their art and their way of life. Angelina, by contrast, lives with an old, mean, rich uncle, is badly treated and quite unloved. Her deliverance is portrayed energetically by both text and picture, against an authentic Old Italian background. A warm, humorous book.

Aunt Nina and Her Nephews and Nieces   Franz Brandenberg, illus. Aliki   (Bodley Head/Piccolo paperback)

A landscape-shaped book full of the sun and fun of a summer day. On her cat's birthday, Aunt Nina, who has neither children nor husband (one sees her, purposefully writing, in a book-lined study), invites her three nephews and three nieces to come to a party. They spend the day in glorious, inventive play, in basement, attic and in between – ostensibly searching for Fluffy, but in fact demonstrating to the modern child that staying at home can sometimes be 'better than the zoo . . . better than the theatre . . .' The birthday cat is found at last, complete with six brand-new kittens – necessitating a visit to the children's families from Aunt Nina, in due course, bulging basket in hand. *Aunt Nina's Visit* has the energetic six and their co-operative aunt *and* the kittens producing a riotous puppet show. Enjoyment of both books may be tinged with envy – but will certainly be wholehearted.

Avocado Baby   John Burningham   (Cape/Picture Lions paperback)

Most children over four will recognize this story for the ridiculous spoof that it is, and love it despite – or because of – this quality of farce. Everyone likes the idea of an elixir which will transform the ugly into the beautiful, the weak into the strong, the dull into the brilliant. Here, it is the honest avocado pear that not only rescues Mr and Mrs Hargrave's baby from puny ill-health, but transforms it into a super-baby, able to pursue a burglar with a broom brandished on high, hurl a pair of bullies into the pond . . . Burningham's deadpan pictures are part of the secret, but not all. Vicarious satisfaction in the triumph of the unlikely? At all events, it works.

A Baby in the Family Althea (Dinosaur paperback)
A straightforward account of family life and reproduction. Sex differences are described and shown, intercourse explained, and birth presented both in text and illustration. The pictures are clear and colourful, and avoid sentimentality while achieving good taste.

*A Baby Sister for Frances
*Bedtime for Frances both by Russell Hoban, illus. Lillian Hoban (Faber/Hippo paperback)
*Badger's Parting Gifts Susan Varley (Andersen Press/Picture Lions paperback)
*Ben: a Mentally Handicapped Child Victoria Shennan (Bodley Head)
Bossyboots David Cox (Bodley Head)
Assertive heroines are popular these days, but many of the books devoted to their exploits emerge as rather put-up jobs. Not so this early Australian saga; Abigail rings true. She is the prototype of little girls we have all known: small females in whom the line between organizing capacity and downright bossiness is blurred. With plot developed against a pioneering Australian background, bushrangers and all, *Bossyboots* is likely to be as successful with the young as its dauntless young heroine is in the face of mortal danger! The illustrations support superbly.

Black Dolly Charles Keeping (Knight paperback)
This is an 'early' Keeping, newly and sensibly brought back for the enjoyment of modern children. (An old, hard-covered copy in my own library has spanned the years for my family, and always been loved.) Black Dolly, a junk-cart pony, tells her own story in language which is simple but rich: 'I was born where the mountains are dark against the sky, and the cooling rain often falls . . .' Her story, too, is simple, but moving, and gives the sort of insight into the lives of animals which all children need. Charles Keeping's pictures are strikingly beautiful, with a sensitivity which exactly matches his own text. The final page is eloquent in word and picture: 'And then they brought me to live in the green meadows where I had been happy long before.' The eye, the ear and the heart are all nourished by such a book.

The Boy Who Was Followed Home   Margaret Mahy, illus. Steven Kellogg   (Dent/Magnet paperback)

>   Robert is an ordinary little boy to whom an extraordinary thing happens: first one, then two, and ultimately forty-three hippopotami follow him home from school. The pictures make no attempt to be funny; they merely illustrate the text and are detailed, earnest and hilarious. All is well, in the end, Robert thinks . . . (How wrong he is is revealed on the last page.) A great joy, this book.

*A Brother for Momoko   Chihiro Iwasaki   (Bodley Head)

Brown Bear in a Brown Chair   Irina Hale   (Macmillan/Papermacs paperback)

>   The plight of a bear who happens to be the same colour as the chair he lives in is explored in this agreeable story. Maggie, his little girl, sets out to help, but Bear finds his new clothes – and the family pets' derision – rather uncomfortable, and settles for a return to his original bare state. Then Maggie's mother solves the problem by recovering the chair in flowery material. But there's a bit left over; just enough for a dress for Bear . . .! Bear has character, Maggie has warmth and Mother has good intentions, and the pictures are full of colour and humour.

The Bunyip of Berkeley's Creek   Jenny Wagner, illus. Ron Brooks (Viking Kestrel/Puffin paperback)

>   The legendary Bunyip of Australia here takes form and sets out to discover his identity. The gentle creature suffers successive rebuffs before – joy of joys! – *another* bunyip arises 'from the black mud at the bottom of the billabong' to join him. The illustrations reveal craftsmanship of a high order. They are unusual, unearthly and eloquent. An outstanding book.

Burglar Bill   Janet and Allan Ahlberg   (Heinemann/Picture Lions paperback)

>   A rousing story of a cheerful, warm-hearted burglar who steals a 'nice big brown box with little holes in it'. When it proves to contain a baby, Bill is in a quandary – until he is burgled by Burglar Betty who is, of course, the baby's mother. A rollicking romp of a book with considerable text – but such fun that the average five-year-old will love it. The pictures strike exactly the

right note – and Betty and Bill marry, reform and return all
their joint loot.

The Butter Battle Book
Horton Hatches the Egg
The Lorax
The Sleep Book
The Sneetches Dr Seuss (Collins)

This bracket of big books will delight children of school-starting
age and older. Dr Seuss himself has a matchless talent for producing rhyming texts which are not only wildly original, but actually
reveal his own care for people, and the world's woes. *The Lorax*,
for example, has a conservation theme, and *The Butter Battle
Book* is a wicked exposé of the stupidity of war. Words and
picture blend into one in these fine books. Two more titles,
Yertle the Turtle and *Harton Hears a Who* are out of print; but
surely only temporarily.

Crispin and the Dancing Piglet Linda M. Jennings, illus. Krystyna
Turska (Hodder & Stoughton)

This artist's work has an earthy, peasant flavour and is at the
same time polished and elegant. The story has the time-honoured
components: three sons dispatched to seek their fortunes,
each equipped in this case – with an animal of his choice. The
youngest casts himself as a likely simpleton when he chooses a
tiny piglet; but of course, he proves to be the happiest in the
end. There is neither violence nor fear in this charming story.
Love, good luck, good humour and honest endeavour abound.
The whole is a thing of beauty.

Chanticleer and the Fox Barbara Cooney (Viking Kestrel)

It is never too soon for children to become accustomed to well-
tuned prose which has borrowed the flavour of its original, in
this case the medieval earthiness and rhythm of Chaucer's *Canter-
bury Tales*. The story is stirring and Barbara Cooney's illustrations have a startling, glowing quality.

*Christmas in the Stable Astrid Lindgren, illus. Harald Wiberg
(Hodder and Stoughton)

* The Complete Nonsense of Edward Lear Edward Lear (Faber)

Could Be Worse! James Stevenson (Viking Kestrel)

This hilarious story will appeal to the reckless in the over-fours. Mary Ann and Louie think that Grandpa is very dull (and he is) until one morning he explodes into a breathtaking, pell-mell account of what happened to him during the night. An astonishing catalogue of unlikely near-catastrophes will keep eyes popping and mouths gaping. The pictures take off in a wild comic-book gallop which captures the spirit exactly.

Crocodile Teeth   Marjorie-Ann Watts   (Deutsch)

A Dark Dark Tale   Ruth Brown   (Andersen Press/Scholastic paperback)

> *Once upon a time there was a dark, dark moor.*
> *On the moor there was a dark, dark wood.*
> *In the wood there was a dark, dark house . . .*

Everyone must know the old, spine-tingling tale. Here, one is led through house, hall and passage, up stairs and through curtain, all depicted in the best tradition of Gothic horror, to a dark, dark corner of a dark, dark cupboard to a dark, dark box . . . in which an utterly engaging little mouse has made her home: a spick and span, shipshape little dwelling from which she peers in terror at our graceless intrusion. A masterpiece, this matchlessly illustrated book, and one which will encourage by-heart performance after several sessions.

Dear Daddy . . .   Philippe Dupasquier   (Andersen Press/Puffin paperback)

The bottom two-thirds of each double spread in this appealing book depicts the same house and garden through the course of a year. Outside and in, a small girl, her mother and her baby brother pursue their lives as the seasons pass, and the children grow. The top one-third of each opening shows the 'Daddy' of the title conducting *his* life as able seaman aboard a freighter in faraway places; you can find him easily in the panoramic pictures. His hair is as red as his small daughter's. The detail in both home and distant scenes is comprehensive but never dazing; it invites scrutiny and speculation. The little girl's letter is simple and touching: 'Please come back quickly. Love from Sophie.' Daddy, meanwhile, is on his way home. Ultimately the bus drops

him outside the house, and Sophie is off her bike and running!
Diana and Her Rhinoceros   Edward Ardizzone   (Bodley Head/Magnet paperback)

A story at once credible and unbelievable; sensible and absurd; stately and undignified; hilariously funny and deeply serious. Only Ardizzone can do this, and he brings it off to perfection here. Diana has good sense, resourcefulness and serenity. (The Victorians might have seen her as an Example. Feminists will certainly claim her as a Sister.) An enduring book in essence, sadly out of print as I write. Surely a temporary state; the world needs people like Diana!

Doctor De Soto   William Steig   (Andersen Press/Hippo paperback)
Once the reader adjusts to the fact that a dentist who happens also to be a mouse might be unwise enough to agree, however reluctantly, to treat a fox with toothache, the potential for humour of a bone-chilling kind is obvious. William Steig explores it to the full. The tone is one of earnest dignity; Doctor and Mrs De Soto are the soul of dental decorum and the fox struggles with himself, as the temptation to betray his benefactors becomes irresistible. The doctor and his tidy little wife are a perfect pair, and more than a match for their transparently avaricious patient.

*Don't Forget, Matilda!   Ronda and David Armitage   (Deutsch)
*Dogger   Shirley Hughes   (Bodley Head/Picture Lions paperback)
Don't Forget the Bacon!   Pat Hutchins   (Bodley Head/Puffin paperback)

The boy in this story sets out to buy for his mother 'Six farm eggs, a cake for tea, a pound of pears . . .' and is sternly instructed not to forget the bacon. His desperate attempts to remember the list have overtones of those party games in which whispered messages become more and more garbled. Much of the fun is in the pictures, which have this artist's characteristic bright yellows and blues and clear outline. The minimal text lends a deceptive air of simplicity; recognizing the likeness in sound between 'six farm eggs', 'six clothes pegs' and 'six fat legs' is essential to understanding as the muddle increases. If the reader's performance gives emphasis to the separate ideas, five-year-olds will enjoy the joke, and soon 'read' the book themselves.

Don't Forget Tom   Hanne Larsen   (A. &. C. Black)

The Doorbell Rang   Pat Hutchins   (Bodley Head)

One could read this cheerful story to three-year-olds with certain success. But fives and sixes will appreciate the need to divide the cookies Ma has made into increasingly small servings as more and more visitors arrive – and may even attempt the computation necessitated by the influx, themselves. Sam, Victoria and Ma manage impressively welcoming smiles (though their expressions do grow a little bleak as the cavalcade proceeds). In the nick of time, there is Grandma at the door with a gargantuan tray of cookies. 'And no one makes cookies like Grandma!' Colour is brilliant, and extra touches are there for the searching: a few – finally dozens – of muddy footprints on the black-and-white tiled floor, the family cat engrossed in the goings-on, a bike, dolls' pram and skateboard in turn parked in the corner. Warmth, fun – and a little instruction on the side. Excellent stuff!

The Dragon of an Ordinary Family   Margaret Mahy, illus. Helen Oxenbury   (Heinemann)

A rollicking yarn about the acquisition by an ordinary family of a pet dragon. An engrossing experience, for which the illustrations must be held half responsible.

Early in the Morning: A Collection of New Poems   Charles Causley, illus. Michael Foreman, music by Anthony Castro   (Viking Kestrel)

This is a signal book, I feel. Most of the poems are in the time-honoured-tradition of the nursery rhyme, while others stop you in your tracks with their substratum of seriousness. But then, were not most nursery rhymes and playground jingles sober in intent originally, however rousing and farcical they now seem? Here, then, are forty new nursery rhymes, embellished with vigorous and feeling pictures by Michael Foreman. Twenty of the poems have been set to music: a bonus for school use perhaps, but inclined to confuse the nature and purpose of the book. (It could be such a rousing, browsing book for the small child lucky enough to acquire it.) No matter: these are poems which will last, to appear in other people's anthologies, and in many cases no doubt, to become picture books in their own right.

The Elves and the Shoemaker   Brothers Grimm, illus. Paul Galdone (World's Work)

This is possibly the most suitable of all the stories available from Grimm, for young children. The tale is of reciprocal kindness, and is quite unthreatening. A poor shoemaker and his wife are so grateful for the help of two night-visiting elves that they make them each a set of clothes. Freshness and vigour attend Galdone's work, and this cheerful story allows it full rein.

Emmie and the Purple Paint   Dorothy Edwards, illus. Patricia Lamont   (Methuen)

Dorothy Edwards has a sure eye for the misdeeds of the very young; '*My Naughty Little Sister*' stories are entrenched among six- and seven-year-olds. Here, her all-too-recognizable protagonist is four-ish, with all the single-minded and inventive zest of that self-centred age group. Emmie doesn't fancy playgroup membership, but does want to try out some of the activities she happened to notice through her protest-tantrum. Mum gets her there in the end, easily enough . . . The pictures are colourful, detailed and accurately observed, the story genuinely funny.

Ernest and Celestine   Gabrielle   (Julia MacRae/Picture Lions paperback)

The reason a great, lumbering bear plays a father-role to a tiny mouse-girl is not divulged in this book, or the titles which follow it. It does not matter; any author-artist who succeeds in producing a pair of beings, animal or human, who relate as sensitively and humorously as this unlikely pair has my vote. This first book is the most direct. Out walking on a wintry day, Celestine drops her precious doll Gideon (a beaked creature of uncertain species) in the snow. Ernest finds him the following day, but he is damaged beyond repair. Good heart and ingenuity win through of course; but Celestine's reactions throughout, observed but never mentioned, are a masterly evocation. I would not rush to introduce the subsequent titles, though many children will find them for themselves, and love them. With more sophisticated themes, they are all superb – for adults, as well as children.

A Fish Out of Water Helen Palmer, illus. P. D. Eastman (Collins, Beginner Books)

This is an absolutely believable story which rushes along at breakneck speed. A small boy tells the tale: how he was warned by Mr Carp at the pet shop not to overfeed his new fish.

> *So much and no more!*
> *Never more than a spot,*
> *Or something may happen!*
> *You never know what.*

Predictably, he ignores this good advice. As you might expect also, the results are spectacular. Otto grows and grows and GROWS! He outgrows his little bowl, a succession of ever greater kitchen utensils, the family bath, the cellar, the local pool . . .! Police and Fire Brigade, both magnificently co-operative, work frantically against rapidly increasing odds. The little boy himself is splendid and undaunted, and finally comes up with a solution. The illustrations, in racy cartoon style, could not be bettered. A quarter of a century old already, with its glory intact, *A Fish Out of Water* is likely to endure.

The Fisherman and His Wife Mark Southgate (Andersen Press)

This is a simply told, brightly illustrated version of the age-old story. A fisherman catches a fish which offers him a reward for sparing its life. The man is happy with the gold coin he receives, but his wife demands bigger and bigger rewards until finally she overreaches herself – and they find themselves back in their original 'dirty old hut'. The moral is strong; but the action, and the repetitive text, will appeal to children. The book itself is well produced, with endpapers which themselves tell a story.

The Fisherman and the Cormorants Gerald Rose (Bodley Head)

A gentle story of reciprocal help between a fisherman and a large bird, both with a family to feed. Gerald Rose excels in this 'semi-fable' field; his land and seascapes are uniformly well designed, his characters lively and believable and his use of colour, as usual, confident and harmonious.

Five Minutes' Peace Jill Murphy (Walker)

Three-year-olds would certainly enjoy this good-humoured tale of domestic chaos arising from Mrs Large's bid for 'five minutes' peace', but the over-fours will go further towards appreciating its nuances. The Large family are elephants and Mrs Large is not one to mince words or pull punches. 'Because I want five minutes' peace from *you* lot', is her answer, when her children demand to know why she is decamping to the bathroom with her breakfast on a tray. One might expect Lester, Laura and the little one to be forceful by nature and enterprising in action, and so they prove to be. The pictures are beautifully planned and executed; they are simultaneously funny and sympathetic, the characters so true to *human* life that one marvels at their elephantine reality. (Jill Murphy *must* have small children of her own, to be able to appreciate and convey Mrs Large's desperate enjoyment of 'three minutes and forty-five seconds of peace'!)

Five to Eight   Dorothy Butler   (Bodley Head)

Flossie and the Fox   Patricia C. McKissack, illus. Rachel Isadora (Viking Kestrel)

The illustrations for this story are so outstanding that one might be forgiven for buying the book on their account alone. But the story of Flossie and her battle of wills with the crafty and conceited fox has its own integrity; and the richness of the Black language of the American South is no impediment to either reading aloud, or understanding. This is a superbly produced book which, with its fable-like tale and superlative pictures, should endure. For near-sixes, rather than just-fours.

Fourteen Rats and a Rat-Catcher   Tamasin Cole and James Cressey (A. & C. Black/Puffin paperback)

An exercise in viewpoints: upstairs, a nice old lady plans to rid her house of the nasty rats in the cellar. In the cellar, a nice rat family would be happy, were it not for the nasty old lady living above them . . . The illustrations, framed in chocolate-brown borders (with the text similarly framed below) are outstanding. Rich colour and excellent design combine with a funny, tongue-in-cheek tale to create an assuredly successful book.

The Ghost-Eye Tree   Bill Martin, Jr, and John Archambault, illus. Ted Rand   (Julia MacRae)

For the almost-sixes rather than the just-fours, this spooky tale. A small boy and his older sister are sent by their mother, on a wild night, to fetch a bucket of milk from the end of the town. Their expedition takes them past the 'ghost-eye tree', and the children obviously enjoy frightening themselves with their wild imaginings. The pictures are spectacularly dark and sinister, the tree itself a ghost with outstretched arms . . . Children, who indulge in this sort of delicious, terrifying self-manipulation, will enjoy the externalization of their fantasies.

The Golden Treasury of Poetry Louis Untermeyer, illus. Joan Walsh Anglund (Collins)

The Goose that Laid the Golden Egg Geoffrey Patterson (Deutsch/Piccolo paperback)

This book is unusual, and immediately attractive. The use of an earthy brown as page colour seems appropriate to the old tale, which is here given a country setting. The goose is seen as the pet of an old peasant couple, and this makes its destruction at their hands more immediately distressing than the bird's brisk dispatch in the original fable. Perhaps the story is none the worse for this; greed is as rampant today as it ever was. The illustrations have life and colour, and the book is beautifully produced.

Gorilla Anthony Browne (Julia MacRae/Magnet paperback)

This immediately attractive book is a satisfying experience, whether or not the point is taken: that a child who longs for her solo parent's companionship and attention can create fantasy situations to meet her need if the real thing is not forthcoming. Here, Hannah's overworked and abstracted father comes up trumps in the end. The last picture in which both are seen from behind, the toy gorilla dangling from Hannah's hand, on their way to the zoo, is heartwarming. 'She was very happy.'

The Great Flood Peter Spier (World's Work)

> High and long
> Thick and strong
> Wide and stark
> Was the ark
> Climb on board

> *Said the Lord*
> *Noah's kin*
> *Clambered in . . .*

and so on, for sixty terse and trenchant lines in three columns, occupying one 'landscape' page at the front of this signal book. (It won the Caldecott Medal in 1978.) A child might well wallow in the wealth of the succeeding nineteen double-spread pages at regular intervals for the whole of childhood, and never be tired of it all. This artist's generosity always overwhelms me. End-papers, title-page – every available space – is adorned with delicate, sturdy, funny, solemn, always pertinent detail. Several almost empty spreads – one depicting a tiny ark on a vast pale blue sea – are breathtaking in themselves, and serve the purpose of slowing the pace and sobering the gaze. Noah and his ark have fascinated children for centuries. Modern youngsters should not be deprived of the vigour, fun and wonder of the old tale. (See also *Noah's Ark*, by Nonny Hogrogian, p. 186.)

Gumdrop: The Adventures of a Vintage Car   Val Biro   (Hodder & Stoughton/Piccolo paperback)

Gumdrop is a real car, who belongs to the author. He is an Austin Clifton Twelve-Four, and was made in 1926. (There are enchanting diagrams of his innards on the endpapers.) Between covers he is given colourful life and real style by Val Biro's jaunty and copious illustrations. Gumdrop has a capacity for trouble which is irresistible; and if you like him you may search out no fewer than seventeen hard-covered picture books, with a sprinkling of paperbacks, and a set of 'Little Gumdrops' for good measure.

*Happy Birthday, Sam   Pat Hutchins   (Bodley Head/Puffin paperback)

Harry and the Digger Lord   Sarah Garland   (Walker)

This book will not be 'like' any other picture book your child is likely to encounter. Sarah Garland wrote and illustrated it on a visit to Australia, and something of that country's size, colour and mystery has crept into it. Harry and his mother 'have come to live' in a cabin, deep in the Australian bush. On a picnic, while his mother searches for rare plants, Harry and Bluey, a rainbow lorikeet who is 'Harry's special Australian friend', stumble upon a herd of kangaroos. Through Bluey's magic, Harry is able to speak with them, but danger looms when the 'Digger Lord's' baby, unnoticed, leaps out of his mother's pouch and into Harry's dilly bag. Accuracy of observed detail, both in text and glorious illustration, makes this a valuable, as well as utterly enjoyable, book.

Helpers   Shirley Hughes   (Bodley Head/Picture Lions paperback) George is a teenage babysitter; clearly known and loved by Mick, Jenny and the baby, Sue, clearly determined to cope, and just as clearly defeated by the children's children-ness and the consequent impossibility of changing anything or reforming anyone. He and they are warm, accepting, loving – and natural. As is Mum, when she returns. George is exhausted . . . but cheerful still. Shirley Hughes creates children who live, breathe, exasperate and delight. A joy of a book.

Hemi's Pet   Joan de Hamel, illus. Christine Ross   (Angus and Robertson) Hemi's class is to have a pet show, and Hemi has no pet. 'What is a pet?' asks his three-year-old sister Rata, and Hemi answers, 'A pet is something that's alive and you love it and look after it.' Rata asks, 'Am I your pet?' and Hemi begins to smile . . . Family relationships are warm and natural in this New Zealand story, and young listener-onlookers are encouraged to think about definitions, as Hemi defends his assertion that a sister *can* be a pet. Predictably, they win a special prize. Christine Ross's illustrations provide evidence of painstaking attention to detail, and succeed in achieving both clarity and elegance.

Hiawatha's Childhood   H. W. Longfellow, illus. Errol Le Cain (Faber/Puffin paperback) Fifty or more years ago, most children learned these particular verses from the long story-poem Hiawatha, by heart. Thirty years ago, they used to spring to my tongue when I needed an off-the-cuff offering – and the short lullaby of old Nokomis was always sung to a tune whose origin had been long lost, even in those days.

Ewa-yea! my little owlet!
Who is this that lights the wigwam?
With his great eyes lights the wigwam?
Ewa-yea! my little owlet!

Errol Le Cain has given the haunting extract inspired treatment. All pages are drenched in the rich deep browns, reds and greens that one associates with the Canadian woods-and-lake landscape, the text set handsomely in edged frames within the greater, totem-embellished borders of the pages. Its certain appeal to adults does not mask the fact that this is a book for children. Hiawatha himself is engagingly small-boyish, Nokomis grandmotherly, the whole warm and joyful.

The Hobyahs Simon Stern (Methuen)
Impossible to capture in words the essence of this old story. The Hobyahs are squat, hideous mini-monsters who are guaranteed to enchant while they horrify. Their determined persecution of 'an old man, an old woman and a little girl' (averted in the end by Little Dog Turpie), is hair-raising in the event, but funny once over. This is a memorable story, encapsulated here in a tiny book. The small, framed, purply-brown pictures and hand-lettered text are just right.

A House is a House for Me Mary Ann Hoberman, illus. Betty Fraser (Puffin paperback)
A mind-boggling list of houses, realistic and fanciful, turns this wordy book into a read-aloud marathon! Impossible to imagine how much information and how many ideas proceed from book to brain and imagination, during the listening. The rhyming, four-line stanzas induce learning by heart, and the illustrations are copious, detailed and varied. In fact, there seems to be something more to look at and think about at each reading. Not for the faint-winded; but a feast for the hardy, both reader and listener.

The House of Four Seasons Roger Duvoisin (Knight paperback)
It is good to see this old favourite available again after some years. 'Father, Mother, Billy and Suzy drove out one sunny day to buy a house in the country,' we are told at first opening. Alternatives abound, and opinions differ, but a decision is made

in the end. Painting poses problems: what combination of colours? The solution, as here described, is instructive in the extreme, and will have youngsters racing to experiment. But the story stands alone, the fresh detailed pictures supporting the action and outcome with style.

How Babies are Made A. C. Andry and S. Schepp, illus. B. Hampton (Time-Life)

Visually arresting, this book begins with the reproductive details of flowers and moves, by way of chickens and dogs, to human beings. It is honest, in no way coy or falsified, and its approach is simple and scientific. Intercourse is explained and birth shown in the clear, collage-style pictures used throughout the book.

I'm Coming to Get You! Tony Ross (Andersen/Puffin paperback)

The 'loathsome' monster of this story makes its way by spaceship, destroying all 'the gentle banana people,' their 'tiny peaceful planet' and sundry small stars on its way to Earth. Here it seeks out little Tommy Brown (located by radar screen) and already a little scared of monsters. Tommy has had a chilling story for bedtime entertainment, gone to sleep and risen to face a new day by the time the monster arrives – and proves to be approximately one-third as tall as Tommy's shoe! A nice twist; and Tony Ross's vivid pictures have spirit and humour.

*I Will Build You a House Dorothy Butler (ed.) (Hodder & Stoughton)

*I'll Always Love You Hans Wilhelm (Hodder & Stoughton/ Knight paperback)

Jam Margaret Mahy, illus. Helen Craig (Dent/Magnet paperback)

With a wife who is a scientist and three lively children to care for, Mr Castle prides himself on being 'an excellent housefather'. His daily round, described in Margaret Mahy's individual style, is energetic indeed; and he certainly does not intend to let the fast-ripening plums go to waste! Plum jam sets the tone – or perhaps the flavour – of the Castles' life for one whole year, by which time . . . Warm-hearted and funny with overtones of lunacy; in short, vintage Mahy. The pictures are detailed, with touches which extend the text without taking over.

John Brown, Rose and the Midnight Cat   Jenny Wagner, illus. Ron Brooks   (Viking Kestrel/Puffin paperback)
 Domestic devotion between John Brown, a gloriously huge and shaggy dog, and Rose, whose 'husband died a long time ago', is undisturbed until 'the midnight cat' appears in the garden. Rose wants to take him in; John Brown is obstructive. The illustrations are striking; soft, night-time colours reflect the mood faithfully. The domestic interior is scrupulously detailed, the outdoor scenes authentic to the missing fence post. An unusual, important book with an unobtrusive but certain message.

Johnny Crow's Garden
Johnny Crow's Party
Johnny Crow's New Garden   L. Leslie Brooke   (Warne)
 The publisher of these old, individual books has seen fit to re-issue them in engaging editions of 'Peter Rabbit' size; and one can only hope that enough modern parents recall the particular and pointed enjoyment of their wacky verses to ensure their revival – and survival.

> *And the Lion*
> *Had a green and Yellow Tie on*
> *In Johnny Crow's Garden . . .*

> *

> *While the Elephant*
> *Said something quite irrelevant . . .*

The best read-to children are the most articulate, in the end. Here are gently humorous, rhyming descriptions of animals behaving sensibly and nonsensically, adorned by the author's stylish and eloquent black and white, and full-coloured, illustrations. Fortunate children will not miss these superb little books.

The Jolly Postman   Janet and Allan Ahlberg   (Heinemann)
 It is impossible to resist the charm of this book-with-additions – no matter how strong your preference for 'straight' books may be (and I thought mine was inviolable). A cheerful postman sets out on his delivery round. Each second page thereafter is an envelope containing a communication (letter, card, invitation – even a tiny book) of astonishing originality. From *Goldilocks* to

The Three Bears, a letter of apology, with nice touches. '*Mummy says I am a bad girl. I hardly eat any porij when she cooks it . . . Daddy says he will mend the littel chair . . .* From *Hobgoblin Supplies Ltd* to *The Occupier, Gingerbread Bungalow, The Woods*, a brochure offering *Little Bag Pie Mix*, '*The Complete book of Foul Curses*' and a '*matching tie and sock set for the Wizard in your life*'. Design, colour and settings all reflect the standards we are accustomed to, in the work of this splendid author-and-artist team. A wonderful gift, this compact, sturdy little volume.

* The Jumblies (also *The Pobble who has no Toes, The Quangle Wangle's Hat, The Owl and the Pussy-cat*) Edward Lear (Grafton 'Little Books of Nonsense')

* Katie Morag Delivers the Mail
Katie Morag and the Two Grandmothers
Katie Morag and the Tiresome Ted
Katie Morag and the Big Boy Cousins all by Mairi Hedderwick (Bodley Head/Picture Lions paperback)

Leon's Christmas Surprise Niki Daly (Gollancz)

The run-up to Christmas is a testing time in most households, parents preoccupied with preparations, and children in an arrested state of *waiting*. Leon's grandfather adds to his frustration by refusing to let Leo see what he is making, though he is observed rummaging in the dustbin, and sawing the leg off a discarded chair . . . On Christmas morning all is revealed: a beautiful, home-made steam-engine and tender has resulted from Grandpa Bob's clandestine efforts. The cheerful reds and greens of Christmas abound in this exuberant, unpretentious book, in which three generations enjoy Christmas in an unsophisticated way. Adults reading it may even come to see that four-year-olds do not need intricate mechanical toys to make Christmas a time of joy.

Libby, Oscar and Me Bob Graham (Blackie/Picture Lions paperback)

On the first page of this highly entertaining book Emily introduces herself as a master of disguises. Libby and Oscar, cat and dog respectively, aid and abet as Emily rings the changes – through tightrope walker and witch to deep-sea diver and elegant lady. Plenty of suggestions for bored children here, with lots of fun and action. Bob Graham's scribbly pictures are both eloquent and funny.

* *The Lighthouse Keeper's Catastrophe*
* *The Lighthouse Keeper's Lunch*   both by Ronda and David Armitage (Deutsch/Puffin paperback)
*Little Bear   Elsie Holmlund Minarik, illus. Maurice Sendak (World's Work/Puffin paperback)
The Little Girl and the Tiny Doll   Edward & Aingelda Ardizzone   (Viking Kestrel/Puffin paperback)

An exceptional book which defies description. Enough to say that it has a proven capacity to fascinate which transcends its modest appearance; a singular quality which ensures rapt attention from the first page. A tiny doll is dropped into the deep-freeze in a grocer's shop by a child who 'did not care for dolls'. The doll is seen by another child, who undertakes her care at long range. Ardizzone's eye and ear for the concerns of the young are impeccable. Here is perfect pitch and true vision.

*Little Gorilla   Ruth Bornstein   (World's Work)
The Little House   Virginia Lee Burton   (Faber/Faber paperback)
* *Mike Mulligan and his Steam Shovel*   Virginia Lee Burton   (Faber/Puffin paperback)

Impossible to think of these two superlative products of this century's picture-book art, except together (they were both frst published in the early forties).

The first tells the story of a humble little house which began her life '. . . on a little hill, covered with daisies and apple trees growing around . . .' Through endless days, nights, seasons and years, the little house stays the same. But the countryside does not; gradually the landscape is transformed, as first roads, then buildings, then a subway, then an overhead railway, surround and ultimately swamp her. Her deliverance is triumphant; she is discovered by 'the great-great-granddaughter of the man who built the house so well . . .' and towed away '. . . to a little hill, covered in daisies'. The detail is copious and meticulous, the whole a joy. (Out of print, but surely bound to re-surface.)

Mike Mulligan and his steam shovel, Mary-Ann, win all hearts, on acquaintance. Mike cannot bear to discard Mary-

Ann, despite her outdated and outworn condition. In the end, he doesn't have to. The story has tension, climax, warmth and imagination; its message concerns the capacity of goodness and courage to convert spite and greed to its own ranks. Young children ought not to miss it; the illustrations support and extend its impact.

Little Tim and the Brave Sea Captain Edward Ardizzone (Viking Kestrel/Puffin paperback; other titles Oxford/Oxford paperback)

This author-artist's work is superlative; it has no counterpart, though many adults cannot understand its success with the young. Suffice to say that Tim, the boy hero, while prey to all the human frailties and trials (fear, homesickness, despair – even seasickness) is throughout steadfast, courageous, loyal and *ordinary*. Ardizzone has never lost a degree of childlike ingenuousness; and he understands a child's need to see himself as the adults' equal. These are believable if outrageous stories of children behaving as adults. They have warmth, vigour, the assurance of coming home in the end, and the conviction that home, family and friends matter most of all. There are eleven 'Little Tim' books.

*Long Ago in Bethlehem Masahiro Kasuya (A. & C. Black)

Lotta's Bike Astrid Lindgren, illus. Ilon Wikland (Methuen)

Lotta is five, and rather big for her boots. It's her birthday, and she had wanted a bike more than anything else. After all, her big brother and sister, Jonas and Maria, both have bikes ... Her solution is in character and almost, but not quite, wrecks the big day. The pictures in this slice-of-life book have cosiness and colour and just avoid sentimentality. Instead, they achieve a sort of homely virtuosity which is irresistible.

Lucky Hans ed. Elizabeth Rose, illus. Gerald Rose (Faber)

Simple, trusting Hans, on his way home with his wages, is easily tricked into the long series of exchanges which leave him with nothing – except his happiness, and a loving welcome at home. The Roses' version has a comical good cheer about its clear, bright pages which is very refreshing.

*Lucy Loses her Tonsils
*Ruth Goes to Hospital
*Tom Visits the Dentist
*Sally Moves House
*Sam's New Dad   all by Nigel Snell   (Hamish Hamilton/Hamish Hamilton paperback)

Mabel's Story   Jenny Koralek, illus. John Lawrence   (Patrick Hardy/Puffin paperback)

Mabel's story, as told to Grandpa on a summer evening, is a tale to keep anyone from sleep. It concerns Mabel and her friends, Horner ('He's the tall one') and Pinter ('He's round and fat'), the chariot they made out of Mabel's old pram, Pinter's umbrella and 'some nails and things', and their eventful expedition to visit the King of the Snow. Mabel gently swings, and Grandpa, supportive as always ('"Good old Horner, good old Pinter," said Grandpa . . .') rests in an old garden chair. John Lawrence's pictures are in quiet colour, with the sort of carefully drawn detail that this strangely haunting story needs. It ensures total attention. The relationship of old and young is moving, believable, and humorous.

*Madeline (and Madeline and the Bad Hat, Madeline and the Gypsies, Madeline in London, Madeline's Christmas, Madeline's Rescue) Ludwig Bemelmans   (Deutsch)

*Maisie Middleton   Nita Sowter   (A. & C. Black/Picture Lions paperback)

Make Hay While the Sun Shines: A Book of Proverbs   Chosen by Alison M. Abel, illus. Shirley Hughes   (Faber)

A unique book. How many modern children hear the old proverbs used, as did an earlier generation? (Memory, being stirred, comes up with a warm feeling for a father who used to say 'It's no use crying over spilt milk . . .') Shirley Hughes's cheerfully scruffy modern children and adults gazing into shop windows ('All that glitters is not gold'), scrubbing floors ('Many hands make light work'), and landing in unsuspected ponds ('Look before you leap') present modern children with the comfort and security of an older age – and bolster their 'literary' repertoire.

Mog's Amazing Birthday Caper   Judith Kerr   (Collins)
> A masterly achievement, this – an alphabet book which actually is a rousing story. Nothing of the 'baby ABC' to demean the school-starter here, but a fast-moving adventure with zany over-tones which will surely make any age-group sit up, smile and snort. (It must be catching.) The tail of a 'Mad Mouse Monster' is held firmly by an Indian (who infiltrated on the 'I' page). 'Don't nip my nose, you nightmare nibbler!' waffles the mouse monster. 'It has not noticed Nicky with his net', 'Oh! Ooh! Ooops! Outwitted! Outraged! Overpowered!' and so on to Z. The candles on Nicky's cake indicate six as a likely audience, but with Judith Kerr's characteristically clear, colourful pictures, this rousing book has all-age appeal.

Mouse Trouble   John Yeoman, illus. Quentin Blake   (Hamish Hamilton/Puffin paperback)
> A miserly miller beset with mice and a cat who can't cope and whose cause is espoused by the mice, ensure hilarity and im-probability in equal proportions. The rollicking tale is further enlivened by illustrations of virtuosity. One almost feels sorry for the miller!

*Moving Molly   Shirley Hughes   (Bodley Head/Picture Lions paperback)

Mr Archimedes' Bath   Pamela Allen   (Collins/Picture Lions paper-back)
> A tongue-in-cheek spoof on the theory of water displacement commonly attributed to the great mathematician of the third century BC. Here, the hilariously plump, pink Mr Archimedes shares his tub with a kangaroo, a goat and a wombat – and the water swamps the floor. His experimentation with the bemused animals makes for great fun and enables the artist to produce absurdly funny pictures – *and* provides an elementary lesson in science. The text is particularly clear and simple, the book beauti-fully designed.

My Holiday   Sumiko   (Heinemann)
> The same small girl as featured in *My Baby Brother Ned* is now about five. (She can be met again in *My School*, the second of the three books.) Ned himself is an active two- to three-year old;

and the family embark on a holiday, caravan in tow. Events are unspectacular but fun: the children sleep in a tent, make new friends, 'muck about' in a rubber boat, and enjoy a beach barbecue. The same loving attention to detail in illustration is seen here as in the earlier books, with pen, brush and colour all deftly used in the service of clarity and feeling.

A New Coat for Anna Harriet Ziefert, illus. Anita Lobel (Julia MacRae)

The theme of an article of clothing which is seen under construction, from the wool growing on the sheep to completion by tailor or dressmaker, is not new. Here, however, it is given a new perspective; Anna and her mother have survived the war and are very poor. Anna's 'fuzzy blue coat that she had worn for so many winters was no longer fuzzy and it was very small.' There is no money available, but goodwill is to be had in plenty from the farmer, the spinner, the weaver and the tailor, all of whom barter their services for possessions which Anna's mother offers readily. Readers may sense her sadness as loved objects – a lamp, a porcelain teapot – change hands; but Anna's joy is worth it all, and the kindly craftsmen join the fatherless family at a 'little celebration' for Christmas. Anita Lobel's pictures have warmth and expression. They reflect faithfully the rural European background against which the tale is set. This is a whole-hearted book, full of hope for an uncertain future.

* The New Red Bike (and *The Picture Prize*) Simon Watson (Puffin paperback)

The Nickle Nackle Tree Lynley Dodd (Hamish Hamilton/Puffin paperback)

An unusual counting book in which original and spirited verse is complemented by elegant and sprightly pictures.

> *Seven haughty Huffpuff birds with hoity-toity*
> *smiles,*
> *Eight cheeky Chizzle birds in cheerful Chirpy piles.*

The ultimate collapse of the overloaded Nickle Nackle Tree is predictable and amusing.

The Night Before Christmas Clement Moore, illus. Tomie de Paola
(Oxford/Oxford paperback)
> It is fitting that this long Christmas poem should receive the
> attentions of a superlative modern American illustrator, for the
> author was also American. First written in 1822 for his own
> children, and published the following year, this story-poem is
> given new life by de Paola's beautifully designed, vibrantly col-
> oured pictures. A note in the book tells us that the artist used his
> own home in a small New Hampshire village as model, and that
> his borders were based on patchwork quilts owned by his own
> family. Certainly, warmth, care and artistry have gone into the
> making of this book, with satisfying results.

Noah's Ark Nonny Hogrogian (Julia MacRae)
> Elegance and dignity are the first features of this excellent book
> to strike the reader; but its main, most enduring and certainly
> most individual quality is the clarity of its biblical-style text,
> and the way it so perfectly complements the illustrations. Noah
> is established in fascinating detail as
>
> > . . . the son of Lamech,
> > who was the son of Methuselah,
> > who was the son of Enoch . . .
>
> a succession which will delight, as well as intrigue, young lis-
> teners. (You can trace the descent backwards, along the bottom
> of the page, to Adam and Eve.) The Old Testament, with its
> rich and varied stories, is little known to many modern children.
> This book could be an excellent introduction, beginning as it
> does with the Creation. (See also *The Great Flood*, by Peter Spier,
> p. 179).

*Not So Fast, Songololo Niki Daly (Gollancz/Puffin paperback)

The Nutshell Library Maurice Sendak (Collins)
> Four enchanting little books in a slipcase. All children love
> miniature objects, and these tiny volumes are splendid books
> in their own right. There is a counting book, a cautionary tale,
> an alphabet and a book of months and seasons – all distinguished
> by Sendak's singular and pointed use of words, and his in-
> comparably earthy, knowing illustrations. Out of print at the

time of writing, these matchless little books must be kept alive in memory, for they will surely return in a more expansive day.

One Moonlit Night   Ronda and David Armitage   (Deutsch/Puffin paperback)

Tony's Dad assures Sam and Tony that their first night sleeping in the tent in the garden will be great fun. The boys are not so sure, but are duly installed. Parents will be familiar with the ensuing upsets, and everyone will enjoy Dad's difficulties when his plan to provide the boys with support backfires on him. This is an assured and entertaining book from an author and artist who know from experience how family life proceeds. The colours are warm, the characters believable, and the text lively.

Phewtus the Squirrel   V. H. Drummond   (Walker)

This book was first written and illustrated (in black and white) nearly fifty years ago. Reissued, its pictures coloured by its still active author-artist, it has lost none of the spirit and bounce which has always characterized V. H. Drummond's work. Its length and complexity offer some comment on the expected concentration of small children in pre-television days; Julian is clearly about three, and yet the text is substantial. Fortunately, it is full of incident, with unlikely twists which are related so seriously that one cannot doubt their veracity. The new publishers have, sensibly, used a large, clear print face, and every single page rejoices in its share of the expressive, elegant-but-sturdy pictures. The story of Phewtus's extraordinary adventures will certainly appeal to modern four-year-olds.

*Phoebe and the Hot Water Bottles   Terry Furchgott and Linda Dawson   (Deutsch/Picture Lions paperback)

The Quangle Wangle's Hat   Edward Lear, illus. Helen Oxenbury (Heinemann/Puffin paperback)

The Rain Puddle   Adelaide Holl, illus. Roger Duvoisin   (Bodley Head/Puffin paperback)

An apparently simple story; but one which requires an understanding of reflections, and the way they work. A farmyard hen decides that another hen has fallen into a large rain puddle. All the other animals come to see for themselves, and draw predictable conclusions. The action is portrayed clearly, in pictures of pleasing design and robust colour. The animal noises ('Gobble-obble-obble! Snort, snort! Oink, oink!') are certain to delight, even if the point is missed at first.

Rhymes Around the Day Jan Ormerod (Viking Kestrel/Puffin paperback)

This is a satisfying collection of poetry for the young, presented in an individual way. A family comprising twin girls of perhaps four or five, and a small brother who reveals his engaging, messy two-ness at every opening, are seen throughout an entire day between early and late bedroom scenes. During the day they go shopping, dress up, eat a meal, and create domestic mayhem in ways that are familiar, ultimately welcoming Dad home to the cheerful chaos. The rhymes are supportive, rather than central to the action, the illustrations delicate and yet buoyant, and the children real.

The Rich Man and the Shoe-maker   La Fontaine, illus. Brian Wildsmith   (Oxford/Oxford paperback)

This book, and those listed below, are all retellings of fables from the French collector, La Fontaine. Brian Wildsmith's rich, glowing colours have produced books of startling beauty. Texts are simple to the point of sparseness; morals easily divined. These are books to treasure.

Other titles: *The Hare and the Tortoise, The Lion and the Rat, The Miller, the Boy and the Donkey, The North Wind and the Sun*

The Rocking Horse   Juliet Harmer   (Collins)

There has always been something mystically appealing about the real, old-fashioned rocking horse. Here, he is loved, lost and found again. The pictures have a luminous quality; representational, they have a grace and energy which matches the strange story. Why does the unnamed little girl go away? An unsolved mystery tugs at mind and heart, and nudges the imagination.

Rumbelow's Dance   John Yeoman, illus. Quentin Blake   (Hamish Hamilton/Puffin paperback)

This excellent book is rather overlooked, I feel; no doubt because its text is quite lengthy, and the overall effect of quiet, rather than vivid colour may lead to its rejection in the face of more spectacular books in library or bookshop. Once tapped, however, its virtues are quickly apparent. Rumbelow (wonderful name!) sets out on a fine morning to visit his old grandparents. Joyfully, he dances across fields and down lanes, meeting in turn a string of people on their way to market with animals or wares to sell. Each is tired and dejected, but all respond to Rumbelow's exhortation to dance along with him. There is a catchy, repeated refrain, varied at each encounter – and a wonderful party at the end, with Rumbelow's old grandparents dancing a stately measure. 'Soon Rumbelow and the poultry boy and the pig-lady and the organ-grinder and the stocking-woman and the tinker and the flower girl and the farmer and all the animals were waltzing round the room.'

Quentin Blake's singular illustrations spread over every single page, so that the text is never daunting. Pictures and story alike abound with that robust warmth and humour that one has come to expect from this author-artist team. A child will re-member the book and be nourished by its innate message of good cheer and generosity for years; perhaps forever.

Runtle the Pig   Ulf Nilsson, illus. Eva Eriksson   (Methuen)
The thirteenth pig of the litter, Runtle is delivered from certain death by the nick-of-time intervention of Peter, Emma and their Dad. The family – Mum is not in evidence – falls into all the traps familiar to warm-hearted but weak pet owners, before Runtle himself takes action and delivers *them* from tyranny, and himself from an inappropriate existence. The text is consider-able, but engrossing, the pictures funny but sensitive. The whole book has virtuosity, and will be read time and again once known.

The Scruffy Scruffy Dog   H. E. Todd, illus. Val Biro   (Hodder & Stoughton/Carousel paperback)
Everyone likes to witness the triumph of the underdog, and here the victor really *is* a dog. Mind you, one could hardly call him humble; Scruffy is as cheerful and confident in his 'underdog' role as he is in his hour of triumph. The story is genuinely funny, and the brightly coloured, generous pictures totally com-plementary. The social commentary is gentle ('Come along Fifi darling,' said Lady Fitzherbert, 'hold up your paw and shake

hands with the nice man.'), if a little stereotyped, the story itself substantial.

Seventeen Kings Margaret Mahy, illus. Patricia MacCarthy (Dent)

This rhyming story-poem is mesmerizing, mysterious – and utterly memorable. Where are the kings going? Why have seventeen of them assembled for a journey anyway? We never find out.

> *Seventeen Kings, and the heavy night swallowed them,*
> *Raindrops glistened on the elephant's backs,*
> *Nobody stopped them, nobody followed them,*
> *The deep dark jungle has devoured their tracks.*

But all is far from serious; and the obscurity of the setting allows this author's imaginative use of language full scope.

> *Small gay tunesters bright clown-trillicans*
> *Butterflied and fluttered by among green trees*
> *Grey baboonsters, brown gorillicans*
> *Were swinging from the branches by their hairy knees.*

An exercise in elocution! The illustrations complement and decorate; but the text is the thing.

The Sign on Rosie's Door Maurice Sendak (Bodley Head/Puffin paperback)

There are four separate stories about the same group of children in this baffling book (Sendak bypasses adults when addressing children, which he likes most to do). You may think there is no child quite as strange as yours until you meet Rosie, Kathy, Lenny, Pudgy, Sal and Dolly. You will then recognize the uniqueness and the sameness of all children everywhere. This is probably the only book ever written which should be issued by 'the authorities' to all the five-year-olds in the world. You can't afford to let yours miss it.

The Sleeping Beauty Felix Hoffman (Oxford)

Children who are ready for the suspense and wonder of the old story will enjoy this beautiful book. Hoffman's restrained but deeply feeling pictures, in muted, sombre colour, provide children with experience of a very different style from that of most

modern artists. This is a classical version: a book to be treasured.
Stories for Under-Fives
Stories for Five-Year-Olds both by Sara and Stephen Corrin
(Faber/Puffin paperback)
The Story About Ping Marjorie Flack and Kurt Wiese (Bodley
Head/Puffin paperback)

Ping is a duck of originality. His home is a boat on the Yangtze
River to which he must return each night. But one night, he
rebels. His subsequent adventures have become justly famous
since his emergence in 1935. Text and pictures are well integrated
in this sound and satisfying book.

* *The Story of Christmas* Felix Hoffman (Dent)
The Story of Ferdinand Munro Leaf, illus. Robert Lawson (Hamish Hamilton/Puffin paperback)

First published in 1937, the tale of Ferdinand, the gentle bull who
triumphs in the face of aggression, goes from strength to strength.
The black-and-white illustrations evoke Spain, bullfights, and
the impossibility of violence when one of the parties simply won't
co-operate. 'So they had to take Ferdinand home . . .'
A classic which may be overlooked unless especially sought out.

* *Tell Me a Story*
Tell Me Another Story
Time for a Story all by Eileen Colwell (ed.) (Puffin paperback)
* *The Tenth Good Thing About Barney* Erik Blegvad (Collins)
There's a Crocodile Under My Bed Mercer Mayer (Dent)

An earlier book by this well-known author-artist. *There's a Night-
mare in My Cupboard* featured the same small boy as we meet here
– again in his bedroom. This time, he devises an artful scheme to
induce the (rather engaging) reptile which he is certain is hiding
under his bed to come out, follow a food trail down the stairs
and allow itself to be locked in the garage. Back in bed, the
author of the plot starts to wonder how Dad will make out in the
morning . . . The simple, brief text says far more than its sparseness suggests it might; and the illustrations are, again, full of
mock-serious comment, and good humour.

There's a Sea in My Bedroom Margaret Wild, illus. Jane Tanner
(Hamish Hamilton/Nelson paperback)

The artist's strong illustrative style steals the scene immediately, in this eye-catching book; but the story has not only an exciting – and surprising – plot, but also a significance which may well be absorbed, if not consciously understood, by young viewer-listeners. 'David was frightened of the sea . . .' we learn at the first striking double spread, 'but he liked collecting shells.' When the sea later pours out of a large conch shell he has found and learned to listen to, he is not afraid at all, for this sea is 'soft and growly and friendly'. Subsequent pictures, in which his bedroom is flooded and David himself revels in the watery chaos, are magnificent. When Mum and Dad come to investigate, they find David rolling on a totally *dry* floor. But David knows it was true . . . and gathers up his beach paraphernalia and sets off for the water. The 'Read it again!' request is inevitable at the end of such a story.

There's No Such Thing as a Dragon Jack Kent   (Blackie/Blackie paperback)

The assertion of Billy Bixbee's mother that 'There's no such thing as a dragon!' wears a little thin as the baby dragon ('about the size of a kitten' when it first appears in Billy's bedroom) grows and grows. Absurd pictures of Mother lifting the dragon's tail to mop the floor beneath, doggedly making more pancakes as the dragon eats them and, ultimately, being obliged to climb in and out of windows because 'there wasn't a room in the house that didn't have some part of the dragon in it', induce guaranteed delight in reader and listener. In the end, even Mother has to admit . . . Jack Kent uses a semi-cartoon style which contains neither concession to adults, nor patronage to children. This is a rollicking story, superbly presented, and rather overlooked, I fear. I would acquire a copy at all costs.

The Three Little Pigs Erik Blegvad   (Julia MacRae/Picture Lions paperback)

There is perfection in this little volume: of design, of re-telling, of illustration. This artist's work needs to be seen away from the more highly coloured, flamboyant examples of modern picture-book art, for it is quietly superlative. Detailed, finely drawn and delicately coloured, each picture demands close and rewarding examination. This is the original version of the famous story. The first two, incautious, little pigs are eaten, only the third courageous and clever little pig surviving to enjoy his sensibly built brick house. This is as it should be. Why tamper with the good old tales, if the result is to water down the effect of the whole?

The Tiger-Skin Rug   Gerald Rose   (Faber/Puffin paperback)

A truly hilarious story about a dusty, moth-eaten old tiger who manages to pass himself off as a rug in the Rajah's palace. Highly original theme, well-rounded plot and lively, colourful pictures ensure its success with small readers and their parents. He's a *character*, this particular tiger!

Tilly's House   Faith Jaques   (Heinemann/Picture Lions paperback)

An outstanding picture book on a subject which has perennnial appeal for the over-fours. House-or-hut building really enters the scene at this stage; and the appeal of dolls' houses is ageless. Tilly is an oppressed but spirited little kitchenmaid in a Victorian dolls' house, until her moment of rebellion arrives. A decision to find 'a place where I can be free and decide things for myself' launches her into an escape which is documented in detail in the meticulous and charming pictures. The home which Tilly subsequently sets up in the garden shed is evidence of her incomparable ingenuity, resourcefulness and industry. Teddy helps, but is bumbling by comparison. Tilly's achievements are direct reflections of her cosy maxims:

> Where there's a will there's a way.
> Waste not, want not.

A joy for all children lucky enough to meet it – as is the sequel, *Tilly's Rescue*, in which the indomitable Tilly embarks on a rescue mission when Edward, the bear, is lost.

Tiny Tim   Jill Bennett (ed.), illus. Helen Oxenbury   (Heinemann/ Picture Lions paperback)

Twenty well-chosen verses with vigorous, superbly appropriate pictures. Unlike many longer anthologies, this brief collection demands non-stop reading. There is no invitation to gloom or even introspection in the poems; even Charles Causley's 'I saw a jolly hunter' will be seen as funny by reason of its slapstick flavour, long before its message starts to emerge.

* *Titch*

* *You'll Soon Grow into Them, Titch*   both by Pat Hutchins   (Bodley Head/Puffin paperback)

* *To Read and to Tell*   Norah Montgomerie   (Bodley Head)

* *Tomie de Paola's Favourite Nursery Tales*   Tomie de Paola   (Methuen)

The Tomten   Astrid Lindgren, illus. Harald Wiberg   (Viking Kestrel)

A book of unique quality. This is the story of a small Swedish troll, '. . . an old, old Tomten who has seen the snow of many hundreds of winters . . .' who lives at an old farm, deep in the forest. No one has ever seen him, but each night he plods from animal to animal, comforting them, and talking to them in tomten language, 'a silent little language a horse can understand.' Each whole-page picture almost demands to be framed and hung. The mood of the long Northern night shines from these sombre, glowing scenes; and the text is sheer poetry. To be a child is to wonder. How could this evocation of remote serenity *not* bolster and fortify?

> Winters come and summers go, year follows year,
> but as long as people live at the old farm in the
> forest, every night the Tomten will trip around
> between the houses on his small silent feet.

The Trouble with Jack   Shirley Hughes   (Corgi paperback)

This engaging story is simple enough for a younger child – but the message is for a big sister. Jack (about two) almost wrecks Nancy's party, but, after the crisis is resolved, she reflects: 'The trouble with Jack . . . is that as he's my brother I've got to put up with him whatever he's like.' Shirley Hughes's children are, as usual, flesh and blood.

The Truck on the Track   Janet Burroway, illus. John Vernon Lord (Cape/Piccolo paperback)

A mad saga of unrewarded effort. The Barney Bros. Circus

truck is stuck on the railway track. All efforts to move it (both sensible and bizarre) prove fruitless. 'The truck still stuck.' In the end, the feckless band set up camp and wait for the train to come. 'Whack! Tough luck.' The picture of tangled truck and train is indescribable, and so is child reception of this extraordinary book. To miss it at the right age is to be deprived.

Varenka Bernadette Watts (Oxford)

Varenka lived long ago in a little house in one of the great forests of Russia. When war was being waged nearby, she did not flee; she must stay to look after travellers, lost children and animals. Her prayer that God would build a high wall round her little house was answered in a way she could not foresee. The illustrations have a formal, glowing beauty, and are yet, like the story, full of feeling.

The Very Worst Monster Pat Hutchins (Bodley Head/Puffin paperback)

> When Billy Monster was born, his pa said,
> 'My son is going to grow up to be the Worst Monster
> in the World.'
> 'No, he's not,' said Hazel, Billy's sister. 'I am.'
> But nobody heard Hazel.

How Hazel contrives to establish the truth of her assertion, in brief text and energetic picture, makes a good book; and Hazel's clear affection for her monsterish little brother is warmly established.

The Walker Book of Poetry for Children Jack Prelutsky, illus. Arnold Lobel (Walker)

A Welcome for Annie Helen Craig (Walker)

Alfred and Susie are firm friends: partners in crime, actually. When Annie and her family come to live next door to Alfred, he and Susie hatch a plot to 'welcome Annie'. Fortunately it backfires, and all is well in the end. The adults in the piece remain calm, if a little shocked, and Annie reveals herself as a worthy adversary and likely confederate. (Certainly a vigorous example to her sex.) That they are all pigs – drawn with feeling and skill which avoids exaggeration and reflects human reaction deliciously – is a measure of this author-artist's wit and capacity. The endpapers are a bonus.

What Do People Do All Day?   Richard Scarry   (Collins)
They dig and cook and paint and drive and clean and build . . . and in this very large, colourful volume you can watch them doing it. Scarry's busy little animal-people provide fascinating entertainment for the young, either to enjoy alone, or with obliging adult on hand to help.

Where's Julius?   John Burningham   (Cape)
A big book this, providing opportunity for regular inclusion of those colourful, large-canvas paintings which the artist does so well. There is sensitivity as well as exuberance in both story and picture. Julius is seen at the beginning and end of the book having meals with his parents. Between, he is never there – he is '. . . riding a camel to the top of the tomb of Neffatuteum which is a pyramid near the Nile in Egypt . . .', '. . . watching the sunrise from the top of the Changa Benang mountains somewhere near Tibet . . .' or '. . . about to shoot the rapids on the Chiko Neeko River somewhere in Peru in South America'. His serious, ever-patient parents deliver the food they have cooked, diligently. (This, too, is carefully described.) A lovely, wordy, tongue-in-cheek book which will sustain innumerable read-aloud sessions.

Wilfrid Gordon McDonald Partridge   Mem Fox, illus. Julie Vivas (Viking Kestrel/Puffin paperback)
This book speaks directly to adults, particularly those who will not see sixty again; but also to the four-and-overs, who see nothing strange in Wilfrid Gordon's search for old Miss Nancy's memory. There is unusual collusion between text and illustration here, and a true feeling for extreme old age, with its uncanny overtones of extreme youth. The result is an overriding flavour of poignancy and gentle humour. One cannot categorize such a book; but sharing it with the young is a joy.

Wombat Stew   Marcia Vaughan, illus. Pamela Lofts   (Omnibus)
Here is an Australian variation on the 'stone soup' theme. A 'very clever dingo' plans to make

Wombat stew,
Wombat stew,
Gooey, brewy,
Yummy, chewy,
Wombat stew!

He is persuaded by a succession of other animals – platypus, emu, lizard, echidna and koala – that his stew needs all manner of extra ingredients. What matter if the young listener has never before heard of an echidna? Here is her chance to learn! The illustrations have vigour and the characters are likeable.

* *The Young Puffin Book of Verse* Barbara Ireson (ed.) (Puffin paperback)

Conclusion

I hope that this book has gone some way towards convincing you that books are important for your baby and child, and for babies and children everywhere. I hope also that I have conveyed my reasons to you for my belief in books, and given you a true picture of what I feel they can accomplish in the lives of young children.

A great deal is said and written these days about the need to speed up the learning process, to get children's minds ticking over at earlier and earlier ages. It can all sound very serious; quite out of touch with the joy, the bounce and the humour that is the real nature of childhood. Heaven forbid that I should have contributed to this over-sober view of a parent's role!

My hope for children is that they will learn to live richly and well; that each child will use her unique qualities to become a happy, contributing adult.

Every person in the world is unique, and every person is essentially alone. We cannot change this aloneness, but we can reduce its effects. Relationships are the key. We nourish our essential humanity when we make contact with one another.

Forging a close relationship with our own baby is easy. Babies are totally unstinting in their willingness to accept us as fountains of pleasure and support. We will be immeasurably enriched by their uncritical devotion, and they, by our love, in return. But we need things in common. No relationship can survive on a basis of mutual, unquestioning adoration.

For relationships, minds have to engage. Ideas are essential, and books constitute a superlative source of ideas. Books can be bridges between children and parents and children and the world.

There is one overriding requirement, however, if books are to work for children in this way. They have to be successful books, books which will make children sit up and take notice, laugh, and ask 'Why?' Books which will involve them deeply, and lift them out of the here-and-now to a place of wonder. 'Read it again' will always be the highest accolade. Such books exist. I hope that *this* book will help you to find some of them and identify others, and that your own developing relationship with your child will keep you reading them together.

Index

BY THE SAME AUTHOR

Cushla and her Books

The fascinating story of the role of books in the life of a handicapped child.

'The story of Cushla goes beyond our farthest imaginings and belongs in the hands of every parent and primary teacher' – Dr Charlotte Huck

'As Dorothy Butler charts the little girl's development from retarded baby to confident child, one marvels at the degree to which the love of her parents and the "extended family" around her has been reinforced by the secondary life that she has gained from stories' – Brian Alderson in *The Times*

'If anyone back to the wall was trying to defend the function of books in the life of the smallest human being, here is the defence' – Edward Blishen in *The Times Educational Supplement*

Written for Children

John Rowe Townsend

An engrossing survey of stories and style from the Middle Ages to the present day.

Written for Children was first published in 1965. It was immediately recognized as not only a readable and stimulating account of the development of children's books but also an important critical contribution to the subject. This latest edition includes a whole new section on English, American and Australian developments spanning the period 1945–1985.

John Rowe Townsend is himself an acclaimed writer for younger people, and his enjoyable, sensible and sometimes controversial view of the subject will provide teachers, students and parents with an invaluable guide, and will be of interest to any reader who cares about the books that are written for children.

'It will be much appreciated for its deft handling of lists of titles, the accomplished survey of techniques and the practised condensation of judgement' – *The Times Literary Supplement*

Play with a Purpose for Under-Sevens

E. M. Matterson

In this new edition of *Play with a Purpose for Under-Sevens* the author gathers together information about pre-school playgroups which has emerged in the last decade (information obtained from watching, talking and working with mothers and young children) and suggests answers to some of the questions that have arisen.

Elizabeth Matterson includes chapters on natural play materials, providing for physical activity and imaginative play. As she herself says in the last chapter 'Children's early years are vitally important and they need plenty of things and people to play with.'

Be Your Child's Natural Teacher

Geraldine Taylor

Every child can benefit greatly from individual tuition at home. With this in mind, Geraldine Taylor, herself a former teacher, has devised this gentle and flexible programme for the parents of primary school children to help them supplement their child's formal education.

By devoting between fifteen and thirty minutes a day to the teaching of English and arithmetic, parents can expect a marked improvement in their child's abilities, as well as an increased enthusiasm for learning.

'Will be found of immense use' – *Daily Telegraph*

'An enlightened interpretation of what homework can mean for younger children' – *The Times Educational Supplement*

'An overdue and excellent little book' – *Living Magazine*